smuggling operation in U.S. history and subsequently the largest forfeiture of attachable assets in U.S. history.The smugglers were real cowboys .Horsetrainers,breeders and ferriers.The boss,Muscles Foster was the trainer of six-time ACHA,NQHA world champion "Cutterbill",one of the most famous cutting horses that ever lived.This golden palomino was the number one sire of world champion cutting horses in the world.These cowboys incorporated the marijuana smuggling with the horse business which proved to keep the operation under the radar.

The horse business obviously entails the moving of lots of alfalfa hay which was the perfect way of concealing the distribution of marijuana. Forty pound bales of hay to conceal forty pound bales of Columbian Red bud marijuana. These loads were multi-ton,typically 40,000 pounds with a minimum order of 7,500 pounds.Clearly,very few individuals or organization could absorb and move these minimum pound shipments.These cowboys went coast to coast with this premium marijuana. The logistics and distribution was vital to the scale of this type of operation. These cowboys would utilize a network of cowboys coast to coast.The perfect cover,horsemen that hauled multi-ton gooseneck trailer loads of hay.There just wasnít any suspicion of horsemen as it relates to massive marijuana moving.These cowboys distributed more marijuana

than any organization,bar none. The largest dealers were net buyers of the cowboys grass.This sensational story will never happen again,here is why. First, is the Gordon Moore law,technology will double every eighteen months. This has held true. Moore an Intel founder was visionary with this prediction.Even though the setting was in the late seventies and early eighties,we all know how technology has progressed in this relatively short span.The rub of tech is the fact that the cowboys used a fleet of 80-foot shrimp boats to import and smuggle. The Texas gulf coast to Santa Marta,Columbia and back.Some 3,000 miles each way at an average speed of 10-15 knots.No global positioning systems,no high technology that we have today.Just maps and compasses interpreted by these cowboys.Today these shrimp boats would be intercepted by the coast guard cutters utilizing all the technology we have today.Lets ponder the inherent risks associated with round trips to Columbia on leaky shrimp boats,they carried 1.5-2 million in cash in scuba tanks,American shrimp boats in Columbian waters,pirates, FARC rebels that more or less control Columbia,suppliers were always aware that the cowboys were carrying large amounts of cash,6,000 miles across the Atlantic ocean with storms and treacherous seas.Not 100 miles offshore as commercial fisherman endure but 3,000 each way and eighteen days at sea loaded with 40,000 pounds of forty pound bales of marijana and lots of cash.It is amazing that these cowboys didnít drown,get highjacked or just lost without the technology available today.These cowboys had no fear.These cowboys had balls bigger than Jesse James.

This story comes from the horses mouth,the cowboys.I was the personal pilot for Rex Cauble,the multi-millionare rancher oilman that employed these cowboys as trainers and ranch managers.We lived at the headquarters ranch in Denton,TX. These cowboys were friends of mine on the ranch.In fact Muscles would often times have dinner with us. No speculation,no conjecture,from the horses mouth. This true story could never happen again. Just as "Cutterbill" was the last of the cooperbottoms, Rex Cauble was the last of the Texas

COWBOY MAFIA

ROY GRAHAM

ACKNOWLEDGEMENTS
The Cowboys

CHAPTER 1

Why I became a pilot is due to the fascination I always had with acceleration,not so much the speed and G's but the speed differential.The opportunity to meet so many fascinating people is the great upside to aviation. I was reared in a beautiful home outside Waco, about a nine iron from the Bush ranch in Crawford, TX Right in the middle of America. Friends thought that I would grow up and follow my father into the oil business; but that was not to be my destiny. I had different aspirations and goals.I had the need for speed.Through aviation I met some fascinating people.Lots of wonderful relationships over the years.

As a kid I loved to build model airplanes, and I spent lots of time building and flying them, I knew early on that this is what I wanted to do.Ginger was very supportive and she worked like crazy to help me get through all the rigors and amass the hours needed to become a commercial aviator.We married at 18 years old. Ginger was a vital part of my progression and ultimately to the best gig in aviation.The rich corporate scene.With corporate aviation you have the opportunity to meet the movers and shakers.I never imagined I would be so close to the largest marijuana smugglers in U.S.history.A network of horse trainers and breeders.I never would have guessed it,neither did anyone else.No one ever suspected these horsemen to be marijuana smugglers, much less broad based and coast to coast.The largest marijuana smugglers the country has ever seen. The focus was always on the world class cutting horses these cowboys bred and trained. Conventional wisdom just doesn't lead anyone to suspect cowboys of these type activities, however the inherent Nature of the horse business provides perfect cover for moving tons of marijuana or alfalfa hay.These cowboys are in all probability the first and last at the marijuana trade.Years and years undetected and unsuspected. In no uncertain terms these cowboys possessed unusual courage and Toughness. They must have had ice water running through their veins.However it is common knowledge that guys with their background are inherently mentally tough.Most of these Cowboys had been rodeo cowboys earlier in life.Rodeo Cowboys are tough as nails.After knowing these cowboys for years I came to realize the type of mental toughness these type of guys possess.

I began as an instructor and chief pilot for Reed's Air Service, a charter service and flight instruction school in Killeen,Tx.Then on to train the worlds' greatest air force,the United States air force.I was an civilian flight instructor in the T-41 program which is where the fighter pilots begin.The T-41 is an unpressurized trainer jet that looks like a smaller version of the F-16.The T-41 is produced by Cessna and it will haul ass.Incidentally,it has the same nose cone as the Cessna citation which I would eventually fly for Rex Cauble.

After the Air Force job, I was hired by Texas International Airlines (Trans Texas) which became Continental Airlines when Frank Lorenzo began rolling up, consolidating airlines.This union busting management style soon created an atmosphere that I was happy to leave for corporate aviation. Frank Lorenzo was a long-haired, thirty-two year-old Spaniard whom had married into money when he took the management controls of Texas International. Lorenzo would be forced out of the airline business altogather soon thereafter. Lorenzo's wife's family were controlling shareholders, so obviously there was some nepotism in play. In 1988 Frank Lorenzo was named most hated manager by business-week magazine, which was appropriate.In these days management didn't have chapter 11 to use as a business strategy to undermine the labor unions,Lorenzo had to do it the old-fashioned way…become a villain.Now days these airline leaders

Pad the financial numbers to the down-side and threaten going chapter 11 which essentially wipes out the capital base and provides a new start with the union contracts being null and void with a chapter 11 filing.Today chapter 11 has become a business strategy for the commercial airlines.If the financial numbers can be cooked to the upside then clearly they can be cooked to the downside to gain tremendous operating leverage with the once prominent airline labor unions.The unions of today have been deemed ineffective with the advent and proliferation of chapter 11 of the bankruptcy code.An friend in the oil business let me know that Denton multi-millionaire Rex Cauble was needing a pilot as he had just acquired a couple of new corporate airplanes.A King Air Beechcraft and a Learjet. This sounded like an ideal situation for me, plus it would be a welcome change from the grind of commercial aviation.The corporate jets are the most fun to fly.More of a tactile feel,more responsiveness.

Rex Cauble was a Texas legend throughout the oil industry and certainly the horse business. "CUTTER-BILL",Caubles' world champion has DNA from Northern California throughout Canada and all the way to

Australia.Hence,#1 sire of world champion cutting horses.

When I went to Denton to be interviewed for the job, I felt great excitement. I was familiar with Rex Cauble for years, and knew that I wasn't going to be talking to just another businessman. I would be meeting a man who had achieved immense fame and fortune, who owned ranches all over the State of Texas, an astute businessman in horses,oil and cattle whose reputation was irreproachable.

Son of a cotton farmer from Aquilla, Rex had been a roughneck in East Texas before founding Texas drilling and eventually became Chairman of the Houston rodeo and livestock Show.The photo with Rex and John Wayne was taken at the Houston rodeo and livestock show But despite his financial position Rex had always remained unassuming and considerate. He always looked out for people. This was an admirable quality for a guy

with this status and wealth.
In his heyday, Rex rubbed shoulders with prominent politicians and celebrities including John Connally, Ronald Reagan, John Wayne, Dale Robertson, Willie Nelson and many other wealthy oilmen. He owned three four thousand acre ranches in Texas where he ran cattle. His ranch in Denton boasted the world's largest cutting horse arena. He owned Cutter Bill, the world's most famous cutting horse. Cutter Bill's Western Wear - which was the Neiman-Marcus of Western clothes.The rich and the famous shopped at these western wear shops in both Houston and Dallas.

This was to be a very cool flying job.Flying for Cauble was a gig that all aviators would covet.House,car,expenses,great trips meeting folks like John Wayne,Dale Robertson,John Connally and several others.Upon arrival in Mean green country I was confident the job was mine and it was.

I parked outside his office next door to the Western State Bank on University Drive in Denton,Tx. one of several banks owned by Rex Cauble. I walked into with a swagger into the bank building as Rexs' office was adjacent. I found out later he was called "Poppa Bear" - the penultimate father figure. When I walked into his office and sat down, I saw a well-dressed,fit middle-aged man with a slightly stocky build with a warm friendly smile. The walls were covered with pictures of celebrities and civic awards he had been given. All very impressive, just like Rex Cauble him-self. I felt an instant rapport with him the minute we shook hands.

"You're Roy Graham?" he asked? "I heard you can fly anything with wings".I knew then it was on.

I nodded. "No problem. Mr. Cauble."

"Tell me about yourself."

I could see my resume on his desk before him, and realized he wanted to hear it first-hand, not merely read the cold facts off a piece of paper. I knew from my own experience that one usually gets a better idea of a person after some conversation. It isn't only qualifications that count. The personality is often the deciding factor in being hired with the wealthy folks because you do spend lots of time with them. I rattled off my personal history and background. He sat and listened, his eyes gleaming, Obviously Rex Cauble was impressed and he hired me on the spot. We shook hands and I drove to Love Field in Dallas to get acquainted with the fleet of airplanes, a King Aire E-90 Turboprop that had the big engines and seated six passengers, a Learjet 35A and a Cessna Citation.I returned to Houston immediately with the good news and smiles all the way to Humble,Tx. We drove the Airstream motorcoach back the next day and arrived at the Cutter Bill Championship Arena. I pulled around to the back of the massive building. Shae Lynn and J.R.

climbed out and began looking around, enthralled and curious about our new surroundings. Ginger stood with me and gazed over the vast stretches that were the hub of Cauble's financial empire.

"Pretty nice," she murmured. "I think I'm going to like it here."

And we did. After a few days, we moved into a house on Ganzer Road, one of many that were dotted over the ranch. Like all top management of Cauble Enterprises, I was also given a Mercedes Benz. This was all part of the salary for working for this incredibly wealthy man. We settled down to what I anticipated being a very lucrative and pleasant life.

On that first day, we were all a little tired from the drive, and decided to turn in early, as we were moving into he house on Gazner road the next morning.

We had fallen asleep when there was a knock at the door. I opened my eyes, switched on the bedside lamp and glanced at the clock beside the bed. Ginger also woke up and stared around the dim interior of the motor home. "Who the hell can that be?" she grumbled. "It's one in the morning."I'll check it out, baby,I said in a sleepy voice.

I rolled out of bed and went to the door. Outside I saw a man standing, grinning up at me in the light streaming out from the inside. He was dressed in cowboy clothes and Lucchese ostrich boots,this cowboy was authentic,not the drugstore type of cowboy.Muscles was about 5'10 and went about 175.No prima donna here,Muscles was the real deal.

"You Roy Graham, the new pilot?" he asked in a deep voice.I have heard you can fly damn near anything.Rex had told him that,obviously. "Yes. Who are you?"

"The name's Foster. I'm the ranch foreman. People call me Muscles." I chuckled at the inapplicable designation. "I'm also the trainer of

"Cutterbill". "Oh, that's one famous horse",I gleemed. "Muscles replied,yep, #1 sire of world champs." Come on I'll show you around the arena,we'll check on "Cutterbill".As we entered the front of the arena, Trophy cases adorned both sides of the entrance.

This horse received the treatment of a six-time world champ,no doubt.As we entered this Massive facility,I could hear music playing in the background,''I asked Muscles,where is that music coming from?
Oh,that's ''Cutterbill'' listening and prancing''.This champion loves music in the evenings.As we approached the stall,sure enough this horse was prancing in the stall.''Wow,this horse is treated like royalty''.Muscles repied,yep,He's a six-time ACHA,NQHA world champ.''Cutterbill''eats bacon and eggs in the morning and the finest grass and alfalfa throughout the day.Little did I know this Muscles knew grass whether for champion cut-

ting horses or the puffer.Muscles told me emphatically that he loved being around horses and thought that every-one should spend time with horses." They are just so calming,spending time with "Cutterbill",Cutter Wanda,and "Cutter Sue",lowers my blood pres-sure.Muscles was right,they are so tranquil yet powerful.This "Cutterbill" had lean muscle just falling off of him.Lean,thick and happy.It must have been all the sex this horse garnered.Everyday, "Cutterbill" was leaving DNA on the earth,Muscles would say.This Cowboy truly loved this horse.Me having not spent much time around horses this seemed sensational to me,after all I was an aviator.This guy lived and breathed horses.

He turned and lurched off into the darkness. I closed the door and climbed back in bed.

"What did he want?" Ginger asked sleepily.

"He came by to get acquainted, He

was awfully friendly. He is the trainer of "Cutterbill''.We took a quick tour of the arena,That horse was in there listening to music and kinda prancing to the tunes.I've never seen that before."

Muscles said "Cutterbill' eat bacon and eggs for breakfast.

CHAPTER 2

I had only been working for Rex for a short while when I realized this elegant, well-mannered, socially prominent Texas businessman had an overwhelming admiration for Muscles Foster, a womanizing,deep talking, super-star horse trainer, whose talent was his amazing skill in training and breeding horses. But this was understandable. The two men had very similar backgrounds.

Both had grown up in cental Texas as cowboys and roughnecks. Rex could identify with Muscles in many ways. Muscles may have been a prima donna horse trainer, something that everyone was aware of but Muscles was the best because he spent so much time with horses and really enjoyed spending time with the champions in training.Muscles was the top rated cutting horse trainer in the country. He brought Rex a six-time world champion, "Cutter Bill". Muscles had brought a winner to Denton, Texas. This was a feather in Rex's cap, something that made him very proud, and he loved Muscles for adding to his growing reputation in the horse business. He had a man working with him who was the best in his field, and a mutual admiration evolved from their close relationship.Muscles was remarkable around horses.It seemed to that these horses were comfortable around Muscles as well.I suppose they have that sixth sense.

It has been said that Muscles needed a firm, reliable father figure in his life to compensate for the lack of a strong father figure in his own life. His own was absent most of the time,Muscles would recall.

Muscles, Charles Ebert Foster was born in Mineola on June 30, 1929, one of four children. As we got to know each other, he told me he had dropped out of school in the fifth grade as he had great difficulty reading and spelling. Muscles left home two years later and began riding broncs and bulls. As his skills improved, he became very knowledgeable about horses, not only training them, but trading them.

I concluded that Muscles was a born horse trader, a talent stemming from those early years when he was learning all he could about horses as well as managing farm and ranch properties. When Muscles was only ten, his mother took him and his three sisters outside their home and hitched a ride to Dallas to get away from an impossible situation with the abusive father.

Four years later Muscles ran off and joined a rodeo in Oklahoma. His small size was obviously an advantage, and he became a steady winner. One year his earnings put him a few dollars away from the world bull riding championship. Muscles may have been skinny and rough-talking, but he knew horses and he knew how to ride them and train them better than anyone in the country.

Muscles spent some time in the army, achieving the rank of sergeant while he served in the Korean conflict. Shortly after his discharge he married his first wife, who was already pregnant by another man. They were divorced two years later, followed by another trip to the altar that Muscles told me "was a drunken mistake" and that lasted only a short time.

As the years passed, Muscles married a third time, a union that lasted eight years before finally ending. The fact that none of his relationships lasted obviously affected Muscles and sparked many of his problems. The women he married were only after the money he earned from his rodeo riding. Muscles was not about the money.Muscles just adored the women. Muscles felt that with big money, he could hold his women.

After his third divorce, Muscles returned to Dallas to discover that his father had died in the Terrell State Hospital, a haven for mental cases. I suspected that this sad event and experience enabled muscles to get into character when the time came. He may have been a genius at handling horses, horse trading and ranch management, but his drinking and his female problems eventually took their toll. After his third marriage landed on the rocks, he went into serious depression and had to be hospitalized.

I always felt sorry for Muscles. He was a wretched figure of a man. Physically he was not the type that women could ever find attractive, and he knew it; and apart from horses, Muscles worshipped women. Any woman. Every woman. He would be standing, perhaps talking to me or to Larry Dale out on the ranch, and if a woman walked by, he would turn and gape after her, his mouth open, his expression denoting total admiration and longing. And like many men I have known with minimal good looks, he was forced to use other means to spark interest from the opposite sex. Muscles believed that the big money would put him on a level playing with the Les Fullers of the world.

I heard him say once that a woman will seldom turn her back on a man with money. Lots of money, which is what Rex Cauble had. Perhaps this was responsible for a case of hero worship on Muscles' part. Rex embodied everything that this man wished he could be - wealthy, admired, sought after and above all, someone who had only to crook his finger to get a woman. Which was very understandable to a marginal looking fellow like Muscles Foster. Muscles wanted to be a player, not a player-hater. One morning on my daily Muscles check, Muscles and I were at the Hardtwist breeding barn and Muscles joked, Roy, what do men and bank accounts have in common?" I replied, "What's that Muscles?" Without any money in them, they generate very little interest." We both chuckled

The second name that was featured heavily in the marijuana smuggling case was Ray Hawkins, who had a very successful horse farm in Madison, Florida. And the Boston horse farm in Quitman, Georgia.

In 1973, Muscles was ranch foreman at the Diamond K Ranch in Garland, Texas. Ray Hawkins hired him to break and train some horses, a job that took him frequently to Florida. It was there, on Ray Hawkins ranch, that Muscles first became involved in the marijuana smuggling business.

He was one of many cowboys that Ray hired to help offload the grass that had been smuggled by boat into the country and offloaded at various spots along the Florida and Georgia coast. The marijuana was transferred from boats to railroad cars and shipped to Ray Hawkins' Boston Horse Farm in Quitman, Georgia. Up to 50,000 pounds of marijuana would be transported at a time in railroad cars, concealed beneath alfalfa hay.

Muscles became a "mule", one of many who offloaded the marijuana from the boats. These Cowboys certainly weren't paid like mules however, $15,000 for a couple hrs. of off-loading. After two years of this arduous manual work, Muscles approached Ray Hawkins and said he wanted to be more deeply involved. In brief, a bigger piece of the pie...

Ray Hawkins offered him a position in distribution as well as helping procure suitable sites where the marijuana could be offloaded. They would never use the same off-loading site twice. With the exception of Thompson seafood in High Island, Texas. High Island was a smugglers paradise, quiet, quaint. A peninsula that runs 25 miles through the inter-coastal population 450. Also known for bird-watching. Different locations were essential to avoid the authorities possibly moving in and lowering the boom.

Ray introduced Muscles to one of his partners, Carlos San Ramon Gerdes, who was the distinct opposite of the rough-looking Texas horse-trainer. Carlos was the son of a Brazilian engineer in California, a handsome, muscular college-educated man, highly intelligent and resourceful. He had amassed over ten million dollars before he was thirty years old. His contribution to Ray Hawkins' marijuana smuggling operation was not only his consummate managerial skills, but the fact that he had the supplier contacts in Columbia at Bogota and Santa Marta.

Before the DEA cracked down on marijuana smuggling in Florida, Ray Hawkins' smuggling operation had operated successfully for almost four years. Muscles joined the team that together with many others, included Ray Hawkins, Carlos Gerdes and Harry 'The Hat' Hannon who worked for Ray at his Madison, Florida, horse farm.

In their last year of operations in Florida, Carlos instructed Harry 'The Hat' Hannon to find someone who had a possible off-load site, perhaps a secluded dock. He would be paid $100,000.

At a bar in Madeira Beach, Florida, Harry met up with Harry Coursey, who went by the name of Charlie. Coursey claimed he was a cigarette smuggler, which suited Hannon perfectly. A former cigarette smuggler would fit in perfectly with their marijuana operation; but what Hannon did not know was that Coursey was an undercover agent with the Georgia Bureau of Investigation.

It came out in the trial later that Hannon's first meeting with Coursey lasted four hours, during which they talked about the possible site for unloading marijuana which Coursey said he had. Hannon told Coursey that he and his associates wanted to see and inspect the possible offload site. They met later at the Ramada Inn at Richmond Hill, Georgia and proceeded to the site.

They checked the depth of the water, as well as the road leading to the offload site, a small wooden dock way in the woods in a swampy area, reached through a small tidal creek. Hannon discussed putting down heavy plywood and wire to insure two tractor-trailers could back in without sinking into the muddy ground.

A few days later Hannon introduced Coursey to Carlos Gerdes. They were concerned over the amount of police activity on the nearby highways, but Coursey reassured them there was little police supervision of the area.

When they got back to the hotel, Hannon asked for waterway charts and also asked Coursey if he knew of any old farmhouses where the marijuana might be stashed. Their discussions continued, with plans being set for a possible arrival of a load of marijuana in the middle of January. This would give them time to hire a crew for the shrimp boat to be trained to behave like shrimpers so that if the boat was stopped by the Coast Guard or Marine Patrol, they would not arouse suspicion.

Carlos asked Coursey to procure a boat and go out and meet the shrimp boat heading for the site near Savannah, Georgia where the marijuana would be transferred to tractor-trailer trucks equipped with conveyor belts.

Also discussed was the use of marine radios to guide the boat and inform them if the coast was clear. Carlos insisted there were to be no guns or cocaine on the boat, which could create heavier penalties if the boat were boarded by the authorities.

An almost unending list of detailed procedures were confessed by Coursey at the trial, all of which only showed that Carlos had obviously known who Coursey really was, and had been playing games with the undercover agent, sending him on a wild goose chase. The boat loaded with marijuana never docked in Florida, but unloaded Colombian Red Bud at High Island, Texas.

This episode only underscored the fact that the smuggling operation was very efficiently run. Carlos was aware that Coursey was not what he claimed, resulting in misleading information being given him to side-track the authorities. If Coursey's information to the authorities had ever resulted in the apprehension of the boat load of marijuana, he was to get 25% of anything seized. But that never happened because Carlos and his gang were smarter than the undercover agent who was led down the garden path. And if, as so many said, Muscles Foster was crazy, it became obvious that Muscles was a lot smarter than he appeared to be. Maybe not as astute as Carlos Gerdes, but smart enough to amass more than a few million from smuggling marijuana into Florida and Texas.

*

After Rex and I relaxed into a pleasant friendly relationship, we were having a drink together one afternoon when he opened up and without my asking him, he told me how he came to meet Muscles. It was back in 1960 when Rex was a relative beginner in the breeding business. On many occasions he had heard about Muscles Foster through the horse breeding circuit. Muscles was known as the finest horse trainer, bar none.

But Rex's biggest claim to fame in the horse business was six-time world champion Cutter Bill, who was destined to make Cauble Enterprises famous in the horse business. This incredible Palomino stallion sired Cutter Wanda, Cutter Sue, Silver King, Hard Twist and the Great Wimpy, all champions. It is true you can't make a cutting horse out of a jackass.

Cutter Bill was only four years old when Rex met Muscles. While Rex was no neophyte when it came to judging good horseflesh, it was Muscles who recognized the limitless potential in Cutter Bill. Muscles had observed this remarkable horse perform, showing the talent that made him the world champion and setting a record for money earned in a single year of competition. Picking a calf out of a herd of cattle and holding it apart is the fundamental skill of any good cutting horse, and after seeing Cutter Bill in action, Muscles knew this horse was destined for the equine hall of fame.

When Muscles began riding bulls

and broncs in rodeos for very little money, fellow cowboys started calling him "Muscles" as a joke. He weighed barely 130 pounds, had large floppy ears and a face that, as one cowboy said to me, would stop a clock. Yet as a teenager he displayed an uncanny talent for horse trading. He traded his first horse for a $90 cow and a Mickey Mouse watch before he reached puberty. Even at that early age, he realized instinctively that he had a talent for bargaining that developed into an instinctive knowledge of how to buy low and sell high where horses were concerned.

By the time Muscles reached physical maturity, his reputation was firmly established as one of the sharpest traders in the county. Before he was hired by Rex Cauble, several other wealthy Texas families like the Caruths and the Phillipses had used Muscles to buy mares for them. Meeting Rex only meant Muscles had another millionaire client to service.

Why these two men became so close is understandable. It's not uncommon for rich and powerful people to surround themselves with talented individuals, and it was no secret that Rex Cauble liked to surround himself with people who would, in one cowboy's words, "kiss his ass and make him feel good."

Not being a kiss-ass type of guy, I never succumbed to blatant flattery to get Rex's approval. I didn't have to. I earned it through doing a good job for him and our close friendship blossomed out of mutual respect.

He earned mine for his noteworthy achievements in business and his incredible ability to wheel-and-deal; and I earned his because of my skills as a pilot.

After a flight, he would often compliment me on my handling of the aircraft. Rex always gave praise, and it was never faint. I guess he knew that a pat on the back will always engender strong morale. Though I may have started out as just another employee of Rex Cauble's, we wound up becoming good friends. We were always honest with each other, and I have always regarded him as a totally honest man, which is the prime reason I was shocked, horrified and have never believed that Rex was consciously involved in the marijuana smuggling racket with Muscles.

During one of the many talks Rex had with me, he let details of Muscles spill out, almost like a father talking about his wayward son.

"Look, I liked Muscles," Rex told me. "Whenever one of his wives left him he would go completely to pieces. On one occasion, he called on me for help. He was crying on the phone like a baby. He'd always take off to God knows where, then he'd call. I'd have to tell him it wasn't the end of the world. Once, after he said he'd run out of money, I sent him a check for $9,000. He thought this would bring his wife back. It did, but once she got her hands on the money, she took off again."

I admired the willingness of a man valued at way above a hundred million in 1980 to reach out with compassion and understanding, as a father would do, to help Charles Elbert (Muscles) Foster.

Rex also told how, after this episode, Muscles was depressed and had developed a liking for rum and coke. After the depression lifted, he went to train a few horses for William Caruth, who was a Dallas, Texas land mogul. Many of the wealthiest, most prominent horsemen wanted Muscles to train their horses.

"That's when Muscles called on me again," Rex continued, "so I hired him to breed mares and train horses for me. He seemed to really like Denton and a few months later I promoted him and made him overseer of all my ranches around Texas. I guess I realized that Muscles had three qualities. He was loyal and hard-working, which was great, but he was also very emotional, something I had to overlook. Sure I'd often bawl him out, try to shout some sense into his head, but whatever I said didn't seem to affect him. He was the way he was, and nothing was ever going to change that. So I took him as he was. His good qualities were more important to me than his failings. And believe me, there's no one that can match him when it comes to choosing horses and training them."

Whenever Muscles happened to stay in the guest house on the ranch, Rex would stop by every Wednesday and pick up his laundry. Rex was certainly like a father to Muscles. Totally opposite in background, tastes, education and social position, who had such a close feelings for each other. This was but one of many odd aspects of their close relationship. Muscles the ranch foreman and the trainer of a six-time world champion cutting horse.

There was another example of Rex Cauble's generous nature and his never-failing kindness. I remember just before his indictment, he decided to take my wife, Ginger, and myself with him and Mrs. Cauble on a trip to Las Vegas.

We were flying 20,000 feet above Albuquerque, New Mexico, when we heard a distress signal from a Beechcraft Bonanza. The pilot, obviously inexperienced, was apparently unable to fly his instruments and was lost.

"Hey, we have to help these folks," Rex said to me.

We circled a few times and finally heard the pilot.

"I have you in sight. Can you help us?"

I responded affirmatively, and we led the other plane into the Albuquerque airport. Had we not heard his call and rendered assistance, the Bonanza would probably have run out of fuel. This episode only underscored Rex's constant concern for others, and his ever-present caring nature.

*

Muscles himself once confessed to me that Rex could "chew his ass out real good" but despite Rex's reprimands, the man stayed on. Maybe it was because he knew Rex sincerely cared, and he knew however badly he behaved, Rex would never fire him because of his unique skill at training champion cutting horses.

After I was hired to pilot Rex's plane and fly him around the country, there were a few other duties that became part of my job with Cauble Enterprises.

Not long after we had settled into the house on Ganzer Road, Rex took me aside.

"Roy, I'd like you to check on Muscles for me every morning, make sure he's okay and taking care of things."

This became part of my daily routine. I soon realized after a while that while Rex had this symbiotic relationship with the man, he was well aware that Muscles had some women problems. His frequent irrational behavior only confirmed many people's opinion that Muscles was women crazy.

It certainly wasn't a major chore for me to keep tabs on Muscles. Our home on Ganzer Road was a short distance from Muscles' house; so wherever Muscles happened to be each morning, either in the breeding barn or out in the pasture on the ranch, I would check on him to make sure he was taking care of ranch business.

Early one morning I found Muscles in the breeding barn which we called "The Hard Twist." He was supervising the breeding of Cutter Bill, something that happened almost every day.

I walked into the Hard Twist and Muscles grinned at me.

"Cutter Bill's taking care of business," he said. And that business was a very profitable one for Rex. The famous horse sired the most world champion cutting horses on record.

I stood around and chatted with Muscles for a while. I didn't want him to think I was there simply to check up on him, and we got into a discussion about my shrimp business. For several years I had been going down to the Coast and bringing back five hundred to a thousand pounds of shrimp to sell to my pilot friends. This little sideline was an easy way to supplement my income from flying and provide my friends with fresh Gulf shrimp.

"Hey, Roy, how do you get into the shrimp business?" Muscles asked me.

I gave him the details and told him I routinely doubled the money I paid for the shrimp. This was the beginning of Thompson's Seafood. He was most impressed, and wanted to know more, but I had to take off and fly Rex to a meeting in Houston.

The next morning during my daily check on Muscles, I was told Rex had given permission for me to fly Muscles to Port Aransas to learn more about the shrimp business. He wanted to know where I bought the shrimp, which happened to be Emery's Seafood, a major shrimp processor in Seabrook, Texas down on the Gulf Coast.

We climbed in the airplane and took off for Port Aransas. I introduced Muscles to Emery, who briefed him on the proper handling of the shrimp, how every load has to have the water drained frequently, and fresh ice placed on top constantly to prevent spoilage. Nothing will spoil faster than fresh shrimp if it's not kept at the right temperature.

We spent the day down on the Coast before flying back to Denton that evening. I gave no further thought to the matter until a week later when I went to check on Muscles at the Cutter Bill Championship Arena. I saw an eighteen-wheeler standing beside the building. Muscles and three men were standing beside the massive truck. I recognized the cowboys - Willis Judge Butler, Larry Dale Washington and Charles Talkington.

As I walked up, Muscles shouted out excitedly.

"Hey, Roy, lookit the truck I've rented," he exclaimed. "I'm going in the shrimp business. These guys are gonna drive for me."

"Do they know how?" I asked.

"No, but I'm showing 'em."

I stood back watching, scarcely believing that Muscles planned to fill an eighteen-wheeler with shrimp. It became a sideshow after a while as the three cowboys tried to maneuver the truck. They obviously had a lot to learn about driving such a massive vehicle. Muscles and I watched, chuckling at the spectacle.

Charles would always jack-knife the rig when he tried to back it up. Willis Judge and Larry Dale were no better. I remember wondering what would happen when they got the tractor-trailer out on the highway.

About a week after Muscles was playing truck-driving instructor, I was making my daily check on him. As I walked up to the arena, my nostrils flinched and I almost felt like throwing up. There was the most sickening smell coming from a trailer parked by the building; and nothing smells worse than rotting fish, especially shrimp.

I was about to turn and get away from the smell when Rex drove up in his Mercedes 450SL. He leaned out of the car for a moment, sniffing.

"What on God's green earth is that awful smell?" he asked.

He climbed out and went over to the truck; then he turned to me.

"I see Muscles is in the shrimp business," he commented. "I hope you didn't encourage him."

"Nope. It was all his idea."

Rex burst out laughing.

"I just hope Cutter Bill doesn't smell that funk. I'd have a sick horse on my hands."

Rex climbed back in his car and

drove off, laughing loudly, and I went about my business. I estimated that there must have been ten thousand pounds of shrimp in the trailer, and from the smell, it could no longer be called "Fresh Gulf Shrimp."

Later that day, Muscles came to visit me at my house.

"Roy," he said plaintively. "I think I bought some bad shrimp."

I burst out laughing.

"Of course. You didn't you drain the water and put fresh ice on the shrimp."

Muscles hesitated. "But I told Larry Dale and Willis Judge to do that."

"Obviously they didn't," I responded.

Muscles thought a moment, his weather-beaten face screwed up as he pondered the situation.

"Tell you what, Roy," he said finally. "I think maybe we bought too many shrimp. I guess the guys misunderstood what I told them. How 'bout buying ‘em off me for two bucks a pound?"

Tactfully I declined. I suspected Muscles would wind up giving the load away. No one in his right mind would buy shrimp that smelled as bad as that did.

But his first failed attempt did not deter Muscles from going into the shrimp business. The next day he came to me, very excited.

"I just leased a warehouse in High Island, Texas" he said. "I'm starting a shrimp business called 'Thompson Seafood.'"

I stared at him, trying to keep a straight face, and realized that Muscles had to be truly crazy just like most people thought he was. He was starting a business he knew nothing about, and his cowboy helpers knew even less than he did, to say nothing about not knowing how to drive an eighteen-wheel tractor-trailer.

This was one of many instances when Rex's Number One man showed me that he may have been the world's best horse trainer, but Muscles was highly specialized, smart in some things, not so in others. And it was only his skills with horses that had fostered the curious relationship he had with his employer - a relationship that would ultimately be responsible for Rex spending five years behind bars and losing 90 million in attachable assets.

CHAPTER 3

Rex may have socialized with Muscles on the ranch, but beyond the confines of his home in Denton, Rex Cauble rubbed shoulders with the financial elite of Texas, a climb up the social ladder that was enhanced by his ever-expanding business interests.

In the late Sixties, he acquired the McVeen steel company and the Miley horse trailer company in Fort Worth; but his major appeal to the rich and famous stemmed from his Cutter Bill Western World stores, first in Houston, then in Dallas. These clothing stores featured fancy Western clothes at extremely high prices that only the wealthy could afford. The Los Angeles Times dubbed Rex's stores "the Neiman-Marcus of Western wear."

Intent on making his home a showplace, Rex hired an architect to build "the world's largest indoor cutting horse arena in America" - an impressive structure that rose into the sky beside the interstate highway north of Denton.

Rex had told the architect: "I don't want to see a finer horse barn anywhere." Completed on February 1, 1967, the stable had its own show ring and a trophy room for the ribbons and loving cups that his horses won.

On the roof was painted the letters CUTTER BILL CHAMPIONSHIP ARENA, visible only to passengers in aircraft flying over on their way in and out of the Dallas-Forth Worth Airport. In front of the stable was a gilded statue of a palomino stud. The buildings on Rex's ranch rated more than a passing glance, especially the horse barn.

Dale Robertson was a close friend of Rex's, and often accompanied him to horse shows and vacations. Other close friends included governors, industrialists and rich prominent society matrons who flocked to the Cutter Bill championship arena for shows, and a close-up look at the prize palomino that was Rex's pride and joy.

Rex told me that Muscles had brought the undisputed heavyweight champion to Denton, a horse that would rise to become a six-time world champion cutting horse.

During one trip in the KingAire when Dale Robertson accompanied Rex, the famous actor commented that "Muscles Foster is the King of the Hill, bar none."

Rex Cauble enjoyed impressing people with his money, his power and his prestige. It was a way of life for him. Every penny of his immense fortune stemmed from his indefatigable efforts and his remarkable talent for making the right business decisions. For that I admired him, and always will.

After moving to Denton and building the arena, Rex eased his way into the local social scene, where he was accepted without question. Once at the Rotary Club, he exhibited such charm that someone said he should anchor the ten o'clock news. Without a doubt, he became a sought-after resident and fitted into the Denton establishment with such charisma that he quickly made friends and had women eager to meet him.

His trips on his Beechcraft KingAire-3063W and his Learjet 24-B were the focus of much town gossip, with people wondering where he went, and who was along on the trip. Often John Connally accompanied Rex, or Jimmy Davis, the ex-governor of Louisiana or the chairman of North

Texas State University, who were all close friends. Rex became a civic leader, and was active in Ruth Carter Stapleton's children's foundation. Ruth, a sister of former president Jimmy Carter, was a Denton resident and a close friend of Rex's.

I remember being in Rex's office one afternoon before Christmas. Ruth called and asked for a donation of five dollars for each of fifty home-less children.

Rex's reply was typical of his generous nature.

"Five dollars won't buy much of a Christmas present," he said. "I'll give five hundred apiece."

That sort of generosity sparked my lifelong admiration of Rex Cauble. Not many knew this man had grown up as the son of a cotton farmer in Aquilla, Texas, just north of Hillsboro. Rex learned early in life the meaning of a tough day's work.

I was extremely proud to fly for such a man who treated people as equals, something most unusual for a man worth more than a hundred million dollars. He hobnobbed with the rich and famous, yet he was never condescending. He treated people the way he wanted to be treated.

Within a year the Denton business establishment had named Rex to the Board of Directors of the First National Bank.

Having amassed a fortune, Rex was never reluctant to share it. He made large donations to many influential politicians, and including John Connally, with whom he had been close friends back in the Forties - "oil brothers" as Rex said once. When Rex bought his big ranch outside Crockett, Texas, in Leon County, John Connally and his wife Nellie were frequent visitors. Connally also bought Cutter Bill's brother, Duster Bill. Louisiana Governor Jimmy Davis bought Cutter Bill's son, Sunshine Bill.

I once overheard Rex joking with John Connally about Cutter Bill.

"I own the only horse in the world that has ridden the elevator to the fifth floor of the Rice Hotel in Houston," Rex said with a deep booming laugh.

Connally's first run for Texas Governor in 1962 had Rex on board as a campaign coordinator. When Connally became Governor, he appointed Rex as Chairman of the Texas Aeronautics Commission, a minor agency that built small airports. The following year, when some of the governor's friends and business associates invested in Southwest Airlines stock, Rex forced through rulings in favor of the new commuter airline.

Rex also became a member of the Special Texas Rangers, an organization of law-enforcement enthusiasts that included cattlemen, corporate executives and lobbyists. They were allowed to carry guns and badges and even dressed like Texas Rangers. Rex then became a patron of the Department of Public Safety's narcotics division, and hired some of the men for part-time security work. He also let them use his plane, including myself as pilot, and at one time had four ex-DPS agents working for him.

Rex confessed that although he hated drugs and men with long hair, he was intrigued by the violent world these men dealt with. He became an honorary member of the Texas Narcotics Officers Association. Many nights the Denton show barn resounded to music and laughter from parties he threw for them. He would always attend these shindigs dressed in flamboyant Western outfits from his Cutter Bill Stores, jeweled suits and python skin boots, too expensive for any cowhand to wear, but definitely *de rigeur* for a Texas oil baron.

Rex's ranch brought an air of glamorous sophistication to the small country town of Denton. His frequent social gatherings were always attended by the cream of Texas society. He became highly regarded, was always respected and I found him a wonderful man to work for; it was truly a tragic turn of events that his close friend and ranch foreman Muscles Foster was the man ultimately responsible for bringing Rex's world crashing down around his ears.

In the more than fourteen years that Muscles worked for Rex, he was given more and more responsibility until he wound up virtually controlling or at least having access to the entire Cauble empire that included ranches all over Texas, the airplanes, the Cutter Bill stores as well as the Long Branch Saloon in Denton, a nightclub that Rex established to insure Muscles' would have a carefree retirement.

But despite his position, Muscles would never stick around for more a few months at a time. His frequent disappearances would often coincide with Rex's attempts to get him to return to a hospital for treatment of his depression, something that terrified Muscles. He often said after a shock treatment, he would wake up the next day and want to die, he felt so bad.

But rather than go for treatment for his depressed moods, he would run away, hitchhike on the Interstate to any place away from Denton. When this happened, more times than I can remember, there would be a collect call from Muscles and Rex would wire him money to come back. It was truly unfortunate that women had such an impact on Muscles self-esteem despite his proven talents and reputation as a world champion horse trainer. He called Rex "Poppa" and Rex always came through for him despite many almost unforgivable escapades.

On one occasion when he disappeared, Muscles took with him the keys to every lock on the ranch, leaving in the lot nineteen mares that he had bred to three different studs. Getting the breeding straight afterwards was a major problem for Rex. The keys were only returned a few weeks later.

On this occasion Muscles had driven to Georgia in one of Rex's Chevrolet Suburbans and wound up at the ranch of a long-haired cowboy named Ray Hawkins, whom he had first met back in the 60's in Tampa. They met again when Hawkins came to the Cauble Ranch to buy a horse. He was a wealthy man who owned a quarterhorse named Tardy Too. On the occasion of Muscles' visit, Hawkins was playing host to two young men - Carlos Gerdes and Jamie Holland - who had found the key to untold riches by smuggling marijuana into Florida from Jamaica, an underworld activity not uncommon in the Seventies.

Young men living on the Gulf Coast of Florida had realized that the local demand for marijuana could be solved by importing it from Jamaica where grass was plentiful and sold for ten dollars a pound. Gerdes and Holland took a 28-foot boat and returned with their valuable cargo that they unloaded on the docks of a marina in the Tampa Bay area.

In the St. Petersburg area Gerdes soon became known as a young man with money. Being single and wealthy, this handsome young Latin had no shortage of girl friends. Through one of these, he met Jamie Holland, a quiet, sullen and very muscular man. Later Muscles would describe Holland as "healthy" - the distinct opposite of Muscles' small, short and definitely underweight frame. Muscles also met John Ruppel, a distinguished white-haired man in his fifties whose name, together with Rex Cauble's, would surface eventually in the hearing room of a New York grand jury investigating the narcotics underworld.

Despite their initial success in drug smuggling, by 1975 Gerdes and Holland found their operation in serious trouble after the U.S. Government destroyed most of the Jamaican marijuana fields. At the same time, the

State of Florida passed more stringent anti-drug laws, forcing men like Gerdes and Holland to look further afield to Colombia.

When Muscles arrived at Hawkins' ranch, and his position in the Cauble empire became known, Gerdes and Holland quickly put their heads together to hatch a new plan to move their smuggling operation to Texas. Muscles was obviously impressed by these two young drug smugglers, whose take was later revealed to be in excess of ten million dollars.

Unknown to any of them was the fact that an agent in the Georgia Bureau of Investigation had been keeping tabs on Carlos Gerdes. When Muscles arrived, driving the Chevrolet Suburban registered to Rex's Miley Horse Trailer company in Fort Worth, the agent wrote down the license number. This was the first occasion when Rex Cauble's name appeared on Federal agents' records, but it soon surfaced again after Muscles returned to Denton in 1976.

According to Rex, after Muscles came back, he claimed he wanted to get into the shrimping business, as I was.

Rex had no reason not to believe him and contacted a boat broker in Aransas Pass, and told him Muscles would be coming down to talk about buying a shrimp boat.

Not long after Muscles went down to Port Aransas to talk about buying a boat, Gerdes and John Ruppel followed and they wound up buying a steel-hulled shrimp boat called the *Monkey*.

As far as Rex was concerned, Muscles was embarking on a new business venture. No one suspected that the *Monkey* would never bring a load of shrimp into port. Instead it would deliver a cargo far more valuable and infinitely more dangerous.

In retrospect, it is incomprehensible to me that anyone would suspect a man of Rex Cauble's reputation and financial standing of being involved with smuggling marijuana from Bogota, Colombia to High Island Texas on a shrimp boat.

As one of Rex's drilling partners said, "If he wanted to bring in marijuana from Bogota, Colombia, Rex would have sent a Boeing 747 after it. He certainly wouldn't use a shrimp boat that goes ten miles an hour and has to fight thirty to forty-foot seas and whose destination was obvious. Then to pull up to a dock with thirty tons of marijuana on board? That's like smuggling an elephant down Main Street."

Yet it happened, and Muscles Foster became the man responsible for the decline and downfall of Rex Cauble, who, like so many others, found it unbelievable that his close friend and ranch foreman was capable of organizing a major drug smuggling operation. I found it difficult to believe, too, because I often flew Muscles to Tallahassee Florida, which is only about fifty miles from Quitman, Georgia. Rex and I both thought he was going to do horse business; instead he was doing marijuana business with Gerdes and Ray Hawkins. Those years set the stage for the operation moving to Texas.

Hawkins realized a move to Texas would be ideal as Muscles had the keys to all Rex's ranches, where there would be ideal storage places for the shipments of marijuana.

When the *Monkey* came into Orange, Texas, the marijuana was offloaded and driven in 40 foot tractor-trailers to the L.R. Ranch in Meridian, Texas by Larry Dale Washington and Willis Judge Butler. Once it arrived, Muscles and Carlos Gerdes took care of distribution. Later Ray Hawkins testified under oath that he received 5,000 pounds of grass for his part in the operation, which a friend later sold for $250 a pound.

I often flew Ray and Muscles to Las Vegas, never dreaming they went there to launder the drug money at the gambling tables. Like Rex, I never knew at that time that Muscles was involved in smuggling marijuana. I presumed the many flights I took him on were for horse business.

About a year after the *Monkey* pulled into Orange, Texas, another shrimp boat, the *Bayou Blues*, arrived with another load from Colombia. Muscles had plenty of cowboys that would be willing to offload. Mexican Hill was where all the ranch workers lived in Denton, Texas, which is at the Ganzer Road exit not far from the road where we lived on Rex's ranch in Denton.

Muscles agreed to provide the drivers as well as storage space for the marijuana. He was to be paid $200,000. At the trial, Ray testified that he got half the load off the *Bayou Blues*. After offloading, there was still some marijuana left on the boat. Ray loaded it into his trailer and hauled it to the Cherokee Ranch in Valley View, Texas. Ray stated in court that at this time, Muscles was acting "looney."

The next time Muscles saw Ray was in the Long Branch Saloon in Denton when Muscles was talking to two farmers about smuggling marijuana. He also told Ray he was doing cocaine. Ray went outside the bar, called Muscles on a pay phone and told him to come outside. He wanted them to talk privately.

"Why are you telling them about the pot?" he demanded angrily.

Muscles assured him it was okay because the men were friends of his. Ray then asked about the marijuana, and Muscles gave Ray a Mason jar filled with marijuana.

"I got plenty more hidden in the old barn at Mexican Hill," Muscles continued.

Ray testified at the trial that Muscles took him to the barn, dug around and produced a Mason jar filled with marijuana.

These statements from Ray Hawkins tied in with my own experience with Muscles. I remember many times he would tell me about his smuggling operation.

I always ignored these statements because I felt he trying to impress and suffering from delusions of grandeur. I suspect this condition stemmed from his own inadequacies as well as being hooked on fast women. It was in 1972 when Ray Hawkins first introduced Muscles to the smuggling business. The first load Muscles was involved in took place at New Orleans. He was paid ten thousand dollars to help load the marijuana on to trucks.

So one might say Muscles never had a chance. He was hooked not only on the big money coming to him from the smuggling operation, but he was hooked on fast women as well.

I remember Muscles Foster as a truly generous character, and to this day I feel it almost unbelievable that when the trial came up, he was found not guilty by reason of insanity, whereas eighteen months later, Rex Cauble found himself a ruined man facing five years behind bars for something he never did, much less knew about.

CHAPTER 4

Having taken the irrevocable step in becoming involved with marijuana smugglers, Muscles moved along his personal yellow brick road at the end of which he envisioned himself being as rich as Rex with enough money to attract any woman he wanted. Which meant virtually any woman. I truly believe there wasn't a woman alive that Muscles would have turned down, and as long as he doled out money, there probably wasn't a woman who would have turned down Muscles.

In December 1976 Muscles visited his

old friend Willis "Judge" Butler. They had been teenage buddies and had spent time together under the care of Bob Grant, who was part owner of the Mesquite Rodeo. Grant was well respected and loved for the care he lavished on misplaced kids like Muscles.

"I loved Muscles," Willis Judge recalled later. "I would get so mad I could kill him, but we have been down a lot of roads together."

At one time Muscles and Willis Judge had gone into the "lead business" - selling worn-out car batteries to a smelting plant, which salvaged the metal. By the time they met again in 1976, Willis was driving a dairy truck. Muscles was working for Rex, but could never save his money; and Willis knew this. So he was more than surprised when Muscles arrived on the scene with a cashier's check for $15,000 drawn on Rex's bank in Denton. "I'm on my way to Colombia," he told Willis. "I'm setting up a dope deal."

Two months later, in February 1977, Muscles was back in Texas. He called Willis Judge and asked if his old friend could do some "errands" in the Beaumont area.

"I'll pay you $50,000," was Muscles' tempting offer.

Needless to say, Willis Judge accepted. "What do I have to do?" he asked. Muscles told him to drive a tractor-trailer to the Sabine Pass, park and wait with a pair of binoculars to watch for the *Monkey*. When the ship arrived, he was to contact the crew and have them transfer the cargo of marijuana to a tractor-trailer.

However, the first shipment was delayed and the *Monkey* never put in an appearance. After three days Muscles remembered Willis Judge Butler, and hightailed it to the Sabine Pass where he found Willis asleep in the car.

They rotated watches after that, waiting for the ship. When it was Muscles' watch, he walked out to the end of a community fishing pier and stood there, staring out to sea for hours.

After the first day, one of his fellow smugglers suggested he get a fishing rod and pretend to be fishing so as not to arouse suspicion.

Muscles went to a sporting goods store, bought seventeen rods and assorted tackle, and returned to the pier. He sat there for hours, trying to figure out how to put everything together. When I heard this story, I thought to myself: Muscles wasn't the brightest guy in the world, but surely he would have known how to put a fishing rod and tackle together… Obviously not.

When the *Monkey* finally arrived, loaded with 40,000 pounds of marijuana, Muscles went into action. He got rid of the foreman at Rex's Meridian, Texas, ranch in Bosque County, Texas, and Willis Judge Butler drove the tractor-trailer there. Carlos Gerdes handled the distribution and had the buyers waiting. He also kept the books. Everything went off without a hitch. The massive tractor-trailer pulled into the ranch, where dozens of men were waiting with cars and trucks. The marijuana was off-loaded, everyone left and Muscles, Gerdes, Holland and several others in the gang went into Denton, Texas, to celebrate.

They all stayed over with Muscles in the guest house on the Cauble ranch. One morning they all had breakfast with Rex himself. When I heard this, I again wondered how on earth Rex could have sat at the same table with these men and not been aware of what was going on, or at least suspicious. Later he said he thought they were "simply Muscles' friends."

Perhaps he was overwhelmed after Hawkins said he was on the market for some land in Texas. Gerdes and Holland had already bought some land near Gatlinburg, Tennessee where John Ruppel had already built a mountaintop palace. Holland planned to become a rancher. Gerdes announced he was going into organic gardening.

Rex had a ranch for sale in Valley View, Texas, named the Cherokee. Ray Hawkins purchased the ranch and paid a hundred thousand dollars in cash for the down payment. Jamie Holland bought one of Rex's prize bulls to get his own herd started. The cowboys decided to take a trip to Las Vegas, where illegal monies are easily laundered as winnings.

The jaunt to Las Vegas actually began in St. Petersburg. Gerdes and two of his partners chartered a plane to fly to Gatlinburg where they picked up John Ruppel. They transferred to a Learjet and flew to Love Field in Dallas.

Transferring planes again, they boarded the Kingaire. Muscles was the first to board and as I helped him with the luggage, Ray and Karen Hawkins drove up in a new Chevrolet Suburban.

They took out several aluminum suitcases filled with money, placed in the aircraft, and they took off for Vegas. One would presume that everyone was dressed suitably for a visit to the casinos, but Muscles wore his ranch clothes, plus a pair of dime-store glasses hanging on a shoelace around his neck. Muscles carried $500,000 in his Zero-Haliburton briefcase for gambling and clothes shopping, which he certainly needed to do.

Muscles attire was embarrassing to Carlos Gerdes, so Gerdes hired a girl named Cookie, gave her several hundred dollars and she bought Muscles some decent clothes including two silk shirts for $150 each. Muscles wore one of the shirts with his old blue jeans and a new pair of jogging shoes.

Carlos reminded me of Don Juan. Suave

On his return, Muscles began a jogging program, something that prompted amused remarks from all of the Cowboys.

In 1978 Rex threw a charity benefit for Doe Whaley's center. Willie Nelson came to perform, and it was at the Nelson concert that Doc Whaley first met Muscles.

It's strange, looking back, that Muscles got involved in marijuana smuggling when Rex was so violently against anyone using this drug, and often said so. When Mick Jagger of the Rolling Stones went shopping at Cutter Bill's in Dallas, the famous rocker was taken up to the ranch for pictures.

Rex proclaimed publicly that Jagger was a poor example for the nation's youth. He was totally against marijuana, and had some of his best employees take a lie detector test to determine if they had ever used it. Doug Kindy, the president of Cutter Bill's failed the test, Rex fired him. "I've never seen anyone so fanatical against pot," Doc Whaley commented afterwards.

Needing a new manager for his store, Rex hired Les Fuller, the original Marlboro man who was six-foot-three, with a handsome face, and an impressive demeanor plus an established reputation in the clothing business. He had been sales manager for Parade Dress, and was well-liked and admired in the industry. He wore gold bracelets and necklaces, open Western shirts and personified the ideal cowboy. After he came on board, his sales acumen sparked an increase in sales which pleased Rex very much. In fact, as time passed, their relationship became closer and Rex was well pleased with the way Les was helping improve his business.

Rex's highest regard for Les Fuller quickly sparked a competitive friendship between Muscles and Fuller. Les may not have been a real cowboy like Muscles, but he was a good imitation. One year his stallion War Chip won the cutting horse championship just as Cutter Bill had done a decade before. Understandably Muscles envied the Marlboro Man's rugged good looks and his easy way with women.

Les' success in business and with women soon fostered Muscles' envy. Shortly after Les came to work for Rex, Muscles was heard to comment "He'll make a positive difference." It's easy to recall Muscles caused Les Fuller to realize being manager of Cutter Bill's Western World was not the place for him. I suspect Muscles was only envious of this man because his looks and personality embodied everything Muscles wished he had; Les was envious of Muscles because o the stoke (fast money) that Muscles had and had talked about finding a place to offload the Colombian Red Bud Marijuana in huge quantities along the Texas Gulf Coast without arousing suspicion from the authorities.

By good luck or sheer genius, Muscles found one. High Island, Texas. If one ever saw a perfect offload site it was High Island, Texas. A small peninsula community with 450 people that is between Galveston, Texas and Beaumont, Texas. This place is

Hollywood. The perfect, quiet set-ting. Smuggling and bird-watching is High Island, Texas.

CHAPTER 5

Realizing that the most dangerous part of any drug smuggling operation was finding a place to unload that would be safe from prying eyes, Muscles took off and searched up and down the Texas coast. Finally he found on a spot near High Island under a bridge that crossed the Gulf Intercoastal Waterway. In this sparsely populated area between Galveston and Beaumont, Texas, he dredged out an inlet. There was ten foot high scrub and weeds on all sides, making it invisible both from the bridge as well as the canal. It was the perfect hideaway. This was where Muscles established the Thompson Seafood Company, a shell corporation for smuggling operations. Thompson Seafood had no refrigeration, incidentally.

As the operation got under way, Muscles and his gang of cowboys had as many as four boats sailing between Texas and Colombia, each one bringing back a cargo of marijuana worth millions. Pot sold in Colombia for $25 a pound. In Texas the price jumped to $250 to $300 a pound.

One of Muscles' hirelings later stated that their landed cost of the pot was about sixty dollars a pound, which resulted in the average load bringing in about five million. And all this was going on without Rex knowing a thing about the operation. As far as he was concerned, Muscles was operating a seafood company, and the ships were bringing in loads of shrimp. Yet Muscles was making a killing… It did not surprise me that Rex didn't know of any of this as he was occupied with his oil and gas, ranching, and civic duties. Rex didn't spend time on his ranches.

With so much money, and without any fear of being apprehended, Muscles a happy man. Muscles had wine, women and song.

He took off for Tennessee, where he met a beautiful blonde, Leslie Sprinkles. Smitten for the thousandth time, Muscles brought this woman back to Texas. Muscles showered her with gifts, jewelry and whatever she wanted. He also gave her a $17,000 flesh-colored Cadillac that was kept in the garage to make sure Rex never saw it. Muscles bought this unit in Sherwood, Arkansas to hide the purchase from Rex.

When she questioned how he was able to be so generous, Muscles told her that he was a majority shareholder in Cauble Enterprises. Muscles also told the young woman he was in the Mafia, and was the actual kingpin. Apparently she believed him. She was the only one who believed him.

Looking back on those years, I find myself more than amazed at the shenanigans of Muscles Foster, as well as the success these cowboys had over a long period. As the saying goes, truth is strange than fiction...

*

Meanwhile Les Fuller was having some personal problems, and was under the care of Doc Whaley, who offered good advice.

"Get your life in order and quit being a showboat," he said. "You've got a tough job to do, and you're only Les Fuller, not the Marlboro Man."

Rex was very understanding of the situation, which was yet another example of his constant compassion for his fellow human beings. Les continued work at Cutter Bill's Western World, and the staff was told to be very careful around him. Les was going through a divorce

At this time Federal lawmen began an investigation of Cauble's enterprises. They presented Rex with a series of subpoenas for financial records and other documents. Muscles Foster's name appeared many times in the subpoenas, and Rex finally realized that something was going on, and moreover, that he could be headed for big trouble. The Texas Rangers had already found some marijuana sweepings at one of the Cauble ranches. A possible investigation was dropped, possibly because Rex was one of the principal sponsors of the Texas Ranger Museum in Waco, or because of his long membership in the Texas Narcotics Officers Association. More significantly, with the way the Texas political scene was moving, Rex was a prime candidate for the office of Commissioner of Public Safety. He was a strong supporter of John Hill in his race for governor, and it was rumored that if Hill won the governorship, he would appoint Rex Chairman of the Texas Department of Public Safety. Following the Federal investigation, and his final realization of Muscles' activities, Rex called together all the men who worked with Muscles and fully interrogated them.

Naturally word got back to Muscles, who promptly disappeared. Rex started making inquiries, and one day a ranch hand knocked on his door.

"You found Muscles?" Rex asked.

"Yup. He's hiding out at Les Fuller's place."

Later Les Fuller was questioned by Federal agents.

"On September 23, 1978, Rex Cauble called me into his office," said Les. "He jumped me for being disloyal and hiding Muscles." Rex was always trying to hunt down Muscles. I assume that is why I had to daily check on Muscles duties.

At that meeting strong words were exchanged, and Rex pulled no punches with Les, who threatened to quit, but Rex asked him to stay on because of an upcoming style show in Austin. Before Les left the office, he had the final word.

"When you started all this stuff about Muscles, I didn't know what was coming down but I do know now. I have a lawyer who showed me a letter detailing what was going on. Just be sure nothing happens to me."

Two days later Les cleaned out his desk at Cutter Bill's and left. Oh, the allure of the big, fast, money. He quit the best job he'd ever had. When Willis Butler called him and asked if he wanted to make a boat trip to South America, there was no hesitation on his part. He was 49 years old and wanted the big, fast cash that these Cowboys were knocking back.

Les Fuller accepted and took the step that made him part of the "Cowboy Mafia."

*

Not long after this, the *Agnes Pauline* moved slowly out of Galveston Bay into the open sea. The boat was a handsome eighty-foot shrimper complete with sonar, radar and a lot of expensive navigational equipment and plastic explosives along with the automatic rifles and M-16s.

On board were five individuals: three men and two women. Les Fuller had brought with him a busty cowgirl he had met on the horse circuit - Gloria Davis, a green-eyed blonde with an acid tongue who was madly in love with him. She had stood by him and helped him recover from a lost love, a beautiful Canadian woman who had divorced him a short time earlier. Gloria kept a diary of the trip, and noted that "the three super sailors didn't know how to work the rigging on a shrimp boat."

She and the other woman, named Holly, took care of the galley while the men did their best to steer the ship. It didn't take long for everyone to realize what sort of voyage lay ahead. Gloria wrote in her diary: "The brooms in the closet were flopping around like plastic pennants in a strong wind. Doors were banging open and shut. The portable radio and other items slid off the table. The refrigerator door swung open and spit out five gallons of milk, a bottle of salad dressing, two bottles of orange juice, a jar of strawberry jam and a can of 7-Up. We finally got it all cleaned up and went upstairs to check on the guys. They asked for something to eat, but my stomach wouldn't let me back in that kitchen again. Holly and I headed for the nearest bed after making a stop in the bathroom."

It was a rough trip. Fifteen foot seas and winds that at times reached thirty knots tossed the small craft about for nine days before they reached the shores of Colombia.

Les suffered all the time with kidney-stone attacks. The pump broke down so showers were out of the question. And worst of all, from the moment it hit high seas, the ship began taking on water. The sonar unit had been installed upside down on the hull, the shrimp boat leaked so bad they had to run the bilge pump constantly to keep the boat from sinking.

Yet despite the discomfort, Gloria's diary recorded a rather poetic description of the voyage.

"The first night at sea was a terrific experience. The ocean was calm, the sky was clear and the moon and stars looked as if they were sewn into an endless black velvet canvas like a large pearl centered among a thousand tiny diamond chips."

She and Les stood watch together at the wheel, both so moved they hardly spoke.

Finally they reached their destination and anchored off the Colombian coast in the middle of a storm. A gale was blowing, and in the middle of the night one of the men discovered the anchor line had broken. They were drifting backwards into the rocks, forced irrevocably toward the shore by the forty knot winds. There was nothing to do but steer straight into the face of the storm.

Adding to their discomfort was the fact that for several days they couldn't establish contact with Big Pete, their Colombian connection. They steamed up and down the coastline, waiting for word from him. Finally Big Pete sent word that delivery had been postponed another three days.

Gloria's diary expressed her feelings. "I think it's our bad luck that keeps us going. If we didn't have bad luck, we wouldn't have any."

The cargo was finally ready to be loaded. After midnight Big Pete's boats arrived - large canoes powered by outboard motors. They pulled up on either side of the boat and large bales of marijuana were thrown on the deck. By the time loading was complete, dawn had broken and everyone was totally exhausted.

Gloria wrote in her diary: "The reality of this trip is finally starting to grip me. I sat perched atop the wheelhouse with my shotgun, two boxes of shells and a .38 revolver. It's not the danger that bothered me, it was the way it affected Les. He was like a kid playing cops and robbers." Obviously the former Marlboro Man hadn't counted on such a turn of events, especially one that could land him behind bars for smuggling.

With all the marijuana in the hold, the return trip to Texas was smoother and easier. Although the boat still leaked badly, everyone was in a happier frame of mind. They took pictures of each other, posing on the marijuana bales, holding their weapons. Les looked tanned and healthy, and pointed his weapon at the sunset, posing like he did as the Marlboro Man. For people engaged in a very dangerous game, they seemed curiously unconcerned. They had achieved their purpose, had connected a load of dope worth millions and Les talked about making a second run.

They celebrated Thanksgiving on board, and the women charcoaled seven pound roast. After dinner Gloria took her coffee out on the deck. Again she recorded her feelings in her diary: "The air was nice and cool. When there's no moon out, it's totally black outside. There's no horizon, nothing to divide the sea from the sky. It's almost like you're weightless, floating through a black void." Obviously her feelings for Les sparked a mounting concern over their questionable future.

"If we were to get caught, it would mean we would be separated for a long time. I don't think I could handle that. I love him and need him so deeply. I couldn't live without him. To me, nothing in this world is important enough to risk that. I guess I'm just feeling sorry for myself because he doesn't feel the same way I do."

When their supply of cigarettes dwindled and they began rationing, tempers flew. The "Marlboro Man" was not accustomed to running out of cigarettes! Finally they made it back to Texas six days after Thanksgiving, 1978.

The loaded down shrimp boat passed through Sabine Pass right up to the public docks where they had reserved a spot to unload their shipment.

The 45,000 pound cargo of marijuana carried with it a strong recognizable odor. Once they entered the Port Arthur ship channel, the undeniable smell of Colombian marijuana trailed them. They passed right in front of the Coast Guard station and docked next to some other shrimpers that were refueling at the docks, only two blocks away from the county courthouse in downtown Port Arthur. If the authorities hadn't already been alerted and were waiting for them, that smell would have certainly raised suspicions and resulted in some action. And action there was.

The minute that Larry Dale Washington

and Willis Judge Butler and some of the cowboys arrived with tractor-trailers to unload the boat, a Federal agent jumped into view.

"Stick 'em up."

Agents popped into view everywhere on the dock: customs agents, Treasury agents, DPS narcs, plus the Galveston Sheriff who insisted on being in on the bust even though it was eighty miles away from his jurisdiction.

Those on board realized there was no way out. They were totally surrounded. They had to lie face down on the deck. One of the agents walked over to Les Fuller and stuck a shotgun in his ear.

"Okay, cowboy," he said harshly. "Are you going to give us the big man in Denton?"

Time for Rex Cauble was running out…

CHAPTER 6

On that fateful day when the *Agnes Pauline* pulled into the dock at Port Arthur, the waiting authorities never dreamed that the cargo would be the largest cache of marijuana ever seized in the history of Texas. Federal agents later estimated their haul to have a street value of over $34 million.

The news spread quickly, and within a few hours, back in Denton, Muscles Foster hurried over to Bill Trantham, an attorney known as "The Tarantula" who had an office in the Western State Bank. Right next door was Rex Cauble, for whom he often performed some legal services. Muscles told Trantham that some of his boys were in trouble, handed over $20,000 and told the attorney to go to Beaumont and bail out the cowboys.

Trantham drove all night and upon arrival in Beaumont, he discovered that bail had been set at $1.6 million.

The case fell within the jurisdiction of David Baugh, an assistant U.S. attorney for the Eastern District of Texas who sometimes wore a gold marijuana pin in his lapel. It soon became clear to this ambitious ego-driven Assistant U.S. attorney that this case had far-reaching implications. David Baugh needed this one to justify his existence.

Rumors around the courthouse pointed to the Marlboro Man, Les Fuller, the most high-profile cowboy and the shrimpboat captain, which meant he might be facing ten years in prison without the possibility of parole. This spread concern among the cowboys, who were all referred to lawyers by Trantham in order to set up whatever deal they could to avoid lengthy prison terms.

One by one information spilled out of their mouths, starting with Fuller who did not relish the idea of spending years behind bars. With all the names in place, Baugh issued subpoenas and the parties were brought in, among them Carlos Gerdes, Ray Hawkins and John Ruppel, but not Muscles Foster, who had literally disappeared. Muscles was Whoudini.

A series of Grand Jury investigations ensued. Baugh issued further subpoenas for the records of Rex Cauble's bank, the sale of his horses and all his business enterprises, but not for Rex himself, who was forced to stand by while FBI agents descended on the bank and seized the desired documents.

It was only from newsmen that Rex was able to learn about Baugh's frequent hints about his involvement in the case. David Baugh certainly utilized the media in this case. Headlines blared and stories began appearing in Texas newspapers about the smuggling operation and how Rex Cauble was possibly involved. This is where the misinformation synergy began. This was all that a desperate Assistant U.S. Attorney David Baugh had was the media.

I remember Rex saying that it was clear to him who was behind the rumors, which had obviously come from the courthouse. David Baugh's career with the US. Justice Department was in jeopardy.

"That damn Assistant U.S. attorney wants to nail my hide to the wall," he said disgustedly, a comment I felt fully justified because Rex Cauble had never had any bad publicity in his life. He was too well liked, too respected and had never done anything to warrant adverse stories about him or his business dealings.

It was early December in 1978 when Trantham got a call from Muscles, who was in Memphis and eager to find out what happened to the cowboys. The Tarantula told him to stay where he was and flew up to Memphis to bring him back to Dallas.

Trantham disclosed later that he thought Muscles was truly crazy, especially on the way back when Muscles talked at length on the future of marijuana smuggling.

"No more boats," he told the attorney. "We'll use submarines. I can get a Navy surplus submarine for only a million." Muscles was a tremendous actor, he could have been another Tommy Lee Jones. Tommy Lee Jones, by the same token could have been muscles in that he is an avid horseman, trainer out of San Saba, Texas.

Trantham said later he chuckled at the thought of Muscles in a cowboy hat looking through the periscope of a submarine in the Houston Ship channel. Obviously Muscles' mental condition was highly questionable, so Trantham checked him into the Arlington Neuropsychiatric Hospital under the care of Doc Whaley.

The good doctor pulled no punches. "He was bonkers," he said later, and kept Muscles in the hospital. His whereabouts were kept secret from the authorities, leading to speculation in the Federal Building that Muscles had "been taken care of."

Crazy or not, Muscles was not going to stay in the hospital. He checked himself out and fled to Krum, Texas a small town a few miles west of Denton, Texas where he holed up in a trailer. Later he called Willis Judge Butler and the two men met and discussed the situation.

"We have got ourselves in a hell of a mess," he told Butler. "But you all have families and I ain't got no ties. Since I got you in this jam, put the blame on me. I'm gone."

Muscles disappeared again, and Butler called Jamie Holland and John Ruppel in Tennessee, asking them to repay the money he had spent outfitting the *Agnes Pauline*. Butler made tapes of these conversations that became the principal evidence against Ruppel. At the same time, these constituted the strongest exculpatory evidence for Rex Cauble.

On the tape Holland named Rex as "the big man down there," a statement that Butler denied. However, Butler finally agreed to testify with the rest of the cowboys, naming Muscles Foster as the kingpin in the smuggling operation. It was obviously a very difficult thing for him to do, because Muscles was his closest friend.

The week before the first trial, Butler drove to the Oklahoma border and rented a cabin in a state park. Like Muscles and Les Fuller before him, Butler had reached a point in his life when desperation gave way to total despair.

In the little kitchen in the cabin, he turned on the gas in the oven, lay down on the bed and awaited the inevitable; but he overlooked the fact that the stove had a pilot light.
A half hour later a massive explosion shattered the cabin windows and blew off the roof. Butler survived unscathed, and apart from nausea from the gas, he was in perfectly good health and still able to testify in court.

*

The "Cowboy Mafia" trial began in September, 1979, by which time the government had indicted 29 people. Following the negotiating and plea bargaining, only twelve of those indicted chose to stand trial. The others pleaded guilty or testified for the government or, as in the case of Muscles Foster, simply disappeared. David Baugh had much to say to the jury.
"This is not a marijuana trial," he said. "This is a racketeering trial."

He then proceeded to outline the scale of the smuggling operation, and stated that he estimated that between August 1976 and December 1978, 275,000 pounds of marijuana worth $34 million had been brought into the country.

Actually, it was north of 500,000 pounds. The Justice Department knew of 275,000 pounds.

Those charged with criminal enterprise included John Ruppel, Carlos Gerdes and an Orange shipbuilder named Martin Sneed.

Ray Hawkins, Jamie Holland and seven others including a Louisiana horse dealer and his brother, faced conspiracy charges. Jamie Holland's wife, Beth, was charged with criminal knowledge.

While the defendants were prosecuted by the government, Rex Cauble became the focus of the defense prosecution. Some of the best narcotics lawyers in the country pointed out that the main government witnesses were all Cauble employees. They stressed that Cauble's men had driven trucks filled with marijuana to Rex's ranches around Texas, where the loads were then divided and distributed. They also claimed that these men frequently met to plot and plan their activities, either in Muscles' Long Branch saloon in Denton or in the Cutter Bill apartment on Westheimer in Houston,

Gerry Goldstein, the most renowned marijuana lawyer in Texas, asked the jury: "Has it occurred to you that everyone in this case connected to Cauble is either cooperating with the government or missing?"

The witnesses wanted to follow Muscles' suggestion that he take the blame, but the lawyers turned the focus of their accusations on to Rex. One of the cowboys, Larry Dale Washington, testified that Rex had paid him $5,000 that Muscles owed him, and claimed Rex said he would "take it out of Muscles' money." Two of the cowboys admitted on the stand that Rex had bailed them out of jail and paid for their attorneys; but no one would testify that Rex was involved in the smuggling operation, other than he was aware of what was going on. Rex always helped people.

Ray Hawkins asked: "Why are Cauble employees pulling innocent men into the spotlight?" The answer, "coercion".

Although two of the defendants were acquitted by the jury, and John Ruppel appealed on a mistrial, nine of the twelve were convicted. Later, Judge Fisher overturned the continuing criminal enterprise conviction against Sneed.

Beth Holland and the Louisiana horse dealer were acquitted, and the jury failed to reach a verdict in the case of John Ruppel.

Considering the seriousness of the case, and the ultimate outcome that turned Rex Cauble from multi-millionaire into a broken, almost penniless man, the matter of the Cowboy Mafia T-shirts remains as a major incongruity in the whole event.

It seems sometime during the trial David Baugh received a package at his office wrapped in brown paper and with a return address: Thompson Seafood, High Island, Texas. Inside was a note from the Tarantula, and a yellow T-shirt with a picture of the *Agnes Pauline* loaded down with marijuana sailing across the State of Texas. Above and below were the words: "Cowboy Mafia."

David Baugh's loud laughter was heard all over the Federal building, bringing a crowd of Federal agents and defense attorneys streaming into his office.

Urgent orders were placed by telephone, and within days, yellow T-shirts were seen everywhere, worn discreetly beneath blouses or long sleeved shirts and suit coats. People would pull their shirts aside to reveal the T-shirt beneath and exchange surreptitious chuckles. One reporter covering the case also wore one.

The conspiracy finally hit the headlines when Gerry Goldstein entered his T-shirt as evidence, and the Judge stared at it, totally bewildered at what was turning into a circus.

By this time everyone assumed that Muscles Foster was dead. Carlos Gerdes and another conspirator had refused to testify before the Grand Jury, and were held in contempt of court.

"They're afraid the same thing would happen to them that happened to Muscles Foster," was the explanation from a Federal narcotics agent.

Slowly the stories began spreading that Rex Cauble had killed Muscles, a rumor that I personally found not only ridiculous but demeaning to one of the finest men I have ever known.

Rex was no killer, but rather a life-long ambassador of goodwill. He had helped many people who in no way could help him. He was appreciative and loyal to Muscles for the work and training he did with the cutting horses. Muscles had put Rex on top of the world with his crowning achievement, Cutter Bill, who became a big moneymaker for Rex. His stud fee was several thousand dollars, and he sired many offspring.

Rex was eternally grateful, and always felt sorry for Muscles, especially over his never-ending problems with women. Rex realized that this unfortunate man, unattractive and unsophisticated as he was, just wanted people to like him, especially women.

Although he became the brunt of many jokes, he had everyone's respect in the field of horse training. There was no one better than Muscles for spotting talent and developing cutting horses into champions, as he did with Cutter Bill.

I remember former Dallas Cowboys head coach Jimmy Johnson from Port Arthur, Texas, incidentally, once stated "everyone is treated especially different according to talent and abilities" - a statement that was certainly true of Muscles. His erratic behavior was tolerated because of his immense abilities.

Willis Butler, his longtime friend and member of the Cowboy Mafia, once said, "Muscles could tell you to the dollar what a horse would be worth, and he could sell cattle when you couldn't give beef away."

The only thing Rex Cauble was guilty of was being a father figure to Muscles and always being good to him, perhaps too good; but to suggest that Rex had killed Muscles over his involvement in the marijuana smuggling was ludicrous, and typical of the varied stories that floated around Dallas after the trial got under way. David Baugh, through the media created a misinformation synergy. A dirty, desperate tactic.

I was as surprised as everyone else when we finally learned what happened to Muscles.

CHAPTER 7

Despite rumors to the contrary, Muscles was far from dead. He had fled to Bolivia, gone into the lead pipe business in Santa Cruz and made no secret of his past or his identity. As Bolivia does not extradite anyone for drug offenses, he openly bragged that he was a wanted man. I suspect he got a bang out of his notoriety, something that appealed to his lifelong desire to be more than a superb horse trainer. While this may not have elevated him to the stature of a Rex Cauble, it certainly must have given him a sense of importance. But eventually, inevitably, Muscles' past caught up with him. The DEA illegally extradited Muscles from Bolivia in the hope of coercing him into testifying against Rex because they had almost no substantive evidence to link Rex to the smuggling operation. So Muscles sojourn in Bolivia ended when two policemen arrived on his doorstep and asked him to come into town to "have a talk." Muscles was no dummy, and he knew what was in store for him. He was not taken into town, but wound up at the airport. and flown across the country to La Paz, where an American narcotics agent was waiting for him.

"I minded in a way," Muscles said later, "but in a way I didn't mind." Why should he? News did not reach Santa Cruz very often, and all his life he had wanted to be "someone," and to be "wanted." He was concerned that everyone had forgotten him. Now at last Muscles knew he was a wanted man. "Mafioso Muscles."

En route on the flight to Miami, Muscles confessed to the narcotics agent that he'd done all right in the smuggling game. Upon landing in Florida, he found himself the center of a media event. He was suddenly a celebrity!

"I couldn't believe they'd think those things," Muscles said later. "Mafia racketeering and all that. I couldn't believe they'd think those things of me."

A Federal magistrate set his bond at over a million dollars. Muscles' ego must have burst its boundaries! One million dollars bond for Muscles Foster! At last he was being treated as if he were what he had often boasted he was - the Kingpin of the "Cowboy Mafia."

Muscles Foster's cup was running over… Muscles was now "Mafioso Muscles.

*

While Muscles was hiding out in

Bolivia, John Ruppel was convicted of several charges including continuing criminal enterprise. However, a new judge on the case, Robert Parker, granted Ruppel a third trial because David Baugh had not revealed the terms of a government deal with two of his witnesses.

During the second trial, the defense attorney continued pointing the finger at Rex Cauble, which finally convinced David Baugh to tell the jury that "there was ample evidence to indict Mr. Cauble." This extraordinary statement made in open court clearly indicated that there was not yet enough evidence to indict Rex, something that everyone felt would occur after Muscles returned.

Muscles and Ruppel were tried together. As Ruppel was a millionaire, he hired an expensive attorney, Robert Ritchie. This was not the case with Muscles, who pleaded poverty, forcing Judge Parker to find a court-appointed attorney to represent him. The Judge wanted Muscles to be represented by a good man in court, where David Baugh and Robert Ritchie would be holding forth. Muscles' sisters, who wanted to arrange for his defense, did not like the idea of a court-appointed attorney, and demanded Racehorse Haynes.

It was then that Judge Parker remembered G. Brockett Irwin, who had achieved a good reputation for winning impossible cases. Irwin came on board, after which one of Muscles' sisters called Racehorse Haynes, who surprisingly, told them "If you've got G. Brockett Irwin, you don't need Racehorse Haynes."

The wheels of justice were moving slowly toward the climax of the largest marijuana smuggling case in the history of Texas. And things were beginning to look very grim for Rex Cauble. This was selective prosecution at its finest. The Cowboys had cash and grass, nothing that the justice department could attach under the Laws of (Rico). Rex had attachable assets.

*

The Cowboy Mafia case had turned out to be a big feather in David Baugh's cap. Since it hit the headlines, twenty people had been convicted. Only two relatively small players were acquitted. Baugh's handling of the case had enhanced his growing reputation and his ego had expanded to mammoth proportions. Now all that remained was for him to add the final frosting on the cake: the indictment of Rex Cauble.

Despite my personal feelings about Rex's innocence that were shared by many others besides myself, there was a flood of circumstantial evidence that would make it a tough nut to crack. The news media became Assistant U.S. attorney David Baugh's best and only friend.

The best defense lawyers that Baugh had ever faced had filled the transcripts with references to Rex's involvement. The judge had accumulated facts and details that were certainly

damning but not enough to convict Rex. Rex employed some of these cowboys, that was the extent of it.
But there were two men whose testimony would certainly cinch the government's case. The first was Muscles Foster, who would certainly be convicted. Or so everyone thought. He was charged with seven counts of racketeering, possession of marijuana with intent to distribute and continuing criminal enterprise.

In every trial thus far, witnesses had singled Muscles out as the kingpin, and they could certainly not change their stories. After Muscles was convicted, he would face ten years to life in prison with no parole. He would have to testify against Rex or expect to spend the rest of his life behind bars and probably die in prison.

Baugh's other critical witness was the Marlboro Man, Les Fuller. His previous statement, more than any other, linked Rex to the case. While

Fuller had been strangely absent from the previous trials, Baugh had kept him out of it because he didn't want to tip his hand to Rex. Both the prosecution and the defense had subpoenaed Rex to testify. Baugh called Fuller's attorney and set up a meeting in Dallas.

Which is when fate took a hand in the proceedings. Fuller's girlfriend, Gloria, informed them that Les had flown out of town to Corpus Christi with some business friends. On the return flight, the plane took off with four men on board: Les Fuller, Jim Geders, a Dallas flight instructor; Jim Cole, part owner with Geders in an air charter service; and Steve Ott, a young man who worked for Geders. All four were seasoned pilots. A storm front had passed over Waco, so when the plane failed to arrive in Dallas, a search was begun between Waco and Austin. No wreckage of the plane was found.

At the same time the search was

being done, a Corpus Christi television newsman, Ron Fulton, happened to be listening to a radio scanner. He overheard a Coast Guard transmission about a duffel bag that had been picked up in a shrimper's net in the bay. The name on the duffel bag read: COLE.

This was the first indication that Fuller's plane had never reached Central Texas. Obviously it had gone down after takeoff.

An immediate search was under way, and Cole's son saw his father's body in Corpus Christi Bay near Portland. Next Geder's body was washed up on the shore near the causeway. Ott was found by a shrimper off Port Aransas.

Three bodies were found, but there was a fourth: Les Fuller. Everyone assumed he was dead, and concluded that he had staged the crash to avoid testifying. Gloria would not believe her husband was dead. Ron Fulton broadcast an appeal over the evening news for help in locating Fuller's body.

A boat operator and an electronics expert volunteered to help Gloria with the search. After a harrowing week searching every conceivable area, Les Fuller's body was finally found, bloated and partially eaten by crabs. Gloria identified her husband from the gold ID bracelet on his wrist. The airplane was still missing, and has never been found.

Fate had robbed David Baugh of his ace-in-the-hole, but the judge still had Muscles, who turned out to be the one person whose testimony would bring down Rex Cauble.

CHAPTER 8

Irwin developed two strategies for Muscles' defense. He could face the fact that the case was hopeless and he make a deal with the government. With this in mind, Irwin went to David Baugh before the trial and tried to negotiate a plea, but Baugh would not listen. He needed as much leverage as he could muster to get Muscles to finger Rex Cauble and the threat of life imprisonment was certainly strong enough leverage to make Muscles spill the beans.

The alternative defense was to plead insanity, not an unreasonable idea considering what all the government witnesses had said, plus Muscles' own statements.

Given Muscles' history of depression and hospitalization, a plea of insanity would be an easy way to achieve an acquittal.

But the government was not going to charge Muscles merely with doing something crazy. He was being charged with running the biggest smuggling operation in Texas for three years and raking in a massive amount of money from the operation.

The trial was moved to Marshall, and began on May 23, 1980. David Baugh went over the details from the day the *Monkey* was purchased until the seizure of the *Agnes Pauline.*

Seated at defense table were John Ruppel and Muscles Foster, clad in a Bolivian shirt and blue jeans.

Side by side, they made a thought-provoking contrast - Muscles looking like a trashed out cowboy, and gentle white-haired John Ruppel exuding all the charm and charisma of a successful businessman.

After his retirement, Ruppel had become known in Gatlinburg for his generosity and community service. He had donated land for the new animal shelter and was one of the major boosters of the Fraternal Order of Police. Ruppel's wife, Margaret, was a refined-looking woman and together they exuded total respectability, the type of elderly couple whose personal and public behavior were above reproach.

As the jury listened to the judge describe the smuggling operation, it was clear from their expressions that members of the jury could never imagine the well-groomed, respectable John Ruppel having anything to do with the disreputable cowboy seated beside him.

Irwin began his opening statement with an attack on David Baugh, warning the jury that the Assistant U.S. attorney possessed great ambition. He emphasized that Muscles was no kingpin in the smuggling operation, but rather a "lame pawn" who found himself overwhelmed by circumstances. Irwin drove home the fact that Muscles had twice attempted suicide, and had endured thirty-one trips to the hospital where his brain had been electrocuted a little at a time, resulting in his present mental condition that could be termed "insanity."

"He will not roll his eyes and he will not drool," Irwin said, "but he suffers from anxiety reaction, chronic moderately severe obsessional personality with chronic depressive trends, recurrent reactive depressions with paranoid features, an underlying manic depressive problem probably with a genetic basis. He also suffers from alcohol dependence if not addiction." Muscles foster should have won an Oscar for this acting performance.

As this seemingly endless list of derogatory statements spewed from Irwin's mouth, Muscles sank lower and lower in his chair, obviously feeling embarrassed, ashamed and disconcerted.

Drawing his lengthy opening speech to a close, Irwin concluded with the warning to the jury that "the ghost of Rex C. Cauble will float through this courtroom throughout the trial" and that the prosecutor was only out to get Cauble because of his success, fame and wealth.

But it was no ghost that entered the courtroom as the first witness. It was Rex himself, his large frame exquisitely dressed and looking powerfully impressive. His features were flushed as he spoke barely above a whisper. This was the moment that David Baugh had pictured ever since he became involved in the case.

Baugh asked his name.

"Rex Carmack Cauble," was the response as their eyes met, with Rex staring at the over-confident black prosecutor who had been his adversary and the object of his curses for over eighteen months. "I am 66, and my business is investments."

"Do you know Muscles Foster?" asked Baugh.

"I respectfully decline to answer because of my attorney's instructions."

Rex had hired William Hundley, the expensive Washington attorney who had defended former attorney general John Mitchell.

Judge Parker would not accept this excuse.

"Is the basis for your refusal to answer the Fifth Amendment of the Constitution?"

Rex replied reluctantly.

"Whether you are guilty or not guilty, you are afforded that right," he said firmly.

He later said that taking the Fifth was the hardest thing he had ever done in his life.

There followed what seemed an endless parade of cowboys who repeated the testimony they had given when Baugh questioned them earlier about their involvement with the smuggling operation.

Irwin seldom countered their incriminating statements, but instead used the government witnesses as character references for the defense, a strategy that annoyed Baugh no end.

The cowboys told how stupid Muscles was when he bragged to women, and how he behaved when the women ran off and he went into the hospital, and how changed he was after his release.

"He would go to bed and only sleep about thirty minutes," one cowboy said. "Then he'd be up, walking around and mumbling to himself, and if you were with him, he'd be chewing on his tongue or spitting."

Baugh realized the case was getting out of control. Dr. Littlejohn, the court-appointed psychiatrist, testified that Muscles "lacked substantial capacity from 1976 to 1978, both to appreciate the wrongfulness of his conduct and to conform his conduct to the requirements of the law."

It was at this juncture that Baugh's superior, stony-faced U.S. attorney John Hannah, arrived from Tyler to take over and attempt to break down Littlejohn's testimony.

"Let's assume," he began, "that Mr. Foster coordinated the trucks and drivers to transport marijuana. Could the jury use that as some evidence pointing toward his sanity?"

Littlejohn had no quarrel with this.

"If he was able to function in a supervisory capacity over others," he replied. "Make judgments about deliveries and assigning trucks, and this type of thing - yes, it would certainly affect the way I felt about the way he functioned at that time."

Hannah continued relentlessly.

"And if he managed the activities of at least five people over a period of two years to smuggle marijuana, that would be evidence of his sanity, wold it not?"

"Yes, sir."

"And if he left the country and traveled to Bolivia to escape prosecution, that would be evidence of his sanity, would it not?"

Littlejohn hesitated a moment.

"Well, if he left to escape prosecution that he knew was coming, yes."

Hannah continued with the long list of evidence.

"That he arranged offload sites, that he established a shrimp company using a fictitious name, that he took part in the importation of 275,000 pounds of marijuana in five shipments over a period of two years without being detected by law enforcement officers; and if all of these things were accepted as true, wouldn't the jury have to accept the fact that Mr. Foster was sane?"

Littlejohn agreed that they would. Hannah then put his notes in his briefcase and returned to Tyler. This exchange was devastating to

Irwin, who commented later that when Hannah got through, there was no way to salvage the case.

During Ruppel's defense, Irwin sat at the table and seriously considered a plea bargain on any terms. He really had only two witnesses to call: Doc Whaley, who could confirm a history of Muscles' ongoing mental problems, and Muscles' sister, Joanne Wells.

The Ruppels each took the stand, and both came off as nice normal people, the personification of respectability. Ruppel's defense stated that he enjoyed helping youngsters get ahead in the world, but that some of them had obviously taken advantage of his charity and naivete. Which sounded very weak compared with the complications inherent in Muscles Foster's plea of insanity.

Irwin pressed on and called his witnesses. Doc Whaley told of Muscles' great feelings of inadequacy, his misgivings about his personal appearance and the many occasions when he talked of how ugly he was and how he could never keep a woman because he was too unattractive.

Joanne Wells told the jury about Muscles' early life when their father had died in a state hospital and another sister turned out to be a paranoid schizophrenic.

"Mr. Cauble took care of my brother," she testified. "He not only saw to his dental work, but he sent him to the eye doctor and tried to make him eat properly. He saw to his clothing and once a week he would gather up his clothes and send them to the laundry."

After Muscles ran away because of Leslie Sprinkles, Joanne related how Rex had people looking for him all over the state.

"When Muscles heard that Rex had to go to the hospital," she said, "he came home. We met in Denton and together we went to see Mr. Cauble. We expected a big confrontation.

Instead when we walked in the door, Mr. Cauble's face lit up like a Christmas tree. Muscles asked 'How are you, old man?" and Rex replied 'How do you think I'd be with you running off all over the country?"

Which only underscored the curious love-hate relationship between these two men, something I always found difficult to understand. Each was dependent on the other in ways that defied a rational explanation.

Irwin closed Joanne Wells' testimony by asking what Muscles had talked about doing if he hadn't got caught. She said he told her he planned to go to Iran to free the hostages.

The jury retired at 4:30 p.m. on June 3, 1980 and they reached a verdict just before midnight. John Ruppel was convicted on four counts, although he was acquitted of continuing criminal enterprise. Muscles Foster was found not guilty.

Muscles nodded without any show

of emotion, looked around and asked the marshal if he could talk with his sisters, who had been standing in the spectator section. He appeared so disoriented that the judge called him to the bench.

"Mr. Foster, this verdict means you are a free man," he explained to the bewildered-looking Muscles. "You're free to go."

Muscles thanked him and said he believed he'd got a fair trial; then he turned and walked outside to where Jerry Irwin's Buick was parked. Irwin unlocked the door and they climbed in and gazed up at the stars through the sunroof.

Finally Muscles turned to Irwin.

"How in hell did you do that?" he asked.

Inside the courtroom David Baugh was asking the same question. Of the two witnesses he might have used to convict Rex Cauble, one was dead and the other was crazy.

The entire foundation of Baugh's

case had crumbled with Muscles' acquittal. He would try to rebuild the case but in the eighteen months he had been preparing to indict Rex, his chances of succeeding had never seemed worse.

Was it over? He wouldn't say.

Was Rex guilty? He couldn't prove it. Not yet, anyway.

Muscles Foster, the "kingpin" of the Cowboy Mafia, was a free man. Many of the others involved in the smuggling ring had been convicted and would spend time behind bars, but Muscles could once again come and go as he pleased.

As for Rex Cauble, while nothing happened immediately, Rex knew it would not be long before David Baugh's ego-driven efforts were successful in ending the successful career of one of the most respected and prominent Texas businessmen ever to wheel and deal in the Lone Star State.

*

Looking back on those years

today, many memories rush through my mind, all reinforcing my firm belief that has never varied: that Rex Cauble had never been guilty of smuggling marijuana.

On the wall at Cutter Bill's Western World in Dallas there had been a photograph showing John Wayne, John Connally and Rex Cauble which to me has always exemplified Rex's impeccable status, both socially and financially. Rex was friends with actors, politicians, oilmen, bankers and ranchers. He mixed with the upper crust of Texas society. He was the leading dealer in rhinestone cowboys' clothing and his wealth stemmed from numerous investments, principally oil, banking and ranching. He was an extremely wealthy man long before the "Cowboy Mafia" hit the headlines.

All of which made the Federal indictments totally preposterous. Compared with Rex's world, the smuggling operation was chicken feed.

It had been estimated that

Muscles and his cowboys would clear five million dollars a load if nothing went wrong, which it often did.

Rex would never prejudice his reputation for five million dollars, a sum that he regarded as chump change. All things considered, there was no reason or motive for Rex ever to become involved in smuggling marijuana.

I have always felt that Rex became the victim of selective prosecution by David Baugh, a neophyte assistant U.S. District attorney out to make a name for himself - and this man used to wear a marijuana pin on his lapel before the trial.

I have always remembered how the TCU football program hit the skids in 1986 because of the misdeeds of Chris Farkus and Dick Lowe, who were only guilty of helping a few players who were in need, just as Rex was only guilty of helping his friends, especially Muscles, a world-champion horse trainer whom he loved and cared for like a son.

Rex had every reason to worship Muscles, a man who had brought six world championships to Denton, plus the Lombardi trophy to the Cutter Bill championship arena. Rex felt that his talent as a horse trainer would never condone any illegal activities whatsoever; yet Muscles organized the largest marijuana smuggling ring in the history of Texas, and carved a name for himself as the kingpin of the Cowboy Mafia.

It's odd that many of the men who make the headlines are often physically unappealing, and with attitudes and personalities that can deter them from pursuing close friendships.

Yet none of Muscles' bad characteristics prevented Rex Cauble from becoming his closest friend. Rex was totally won over by Muscles' talent with horses, a talent that brought fame and fortune to Rex, and for this reason the Texas millionaire could never turn his back on this man who worshipped him to such an unfathomable degree.

I shall never forget Muscles. He not only had a feeble psyche but a feeble physique. He weighed no more than 130 pounds dripping wet and had the funniest-looking ears I've ever seen on any man. His lack of good looks led to his low self-esteem which he was always trying to reinforce. He was desperately envious of Les Fuller, the handsome Marlboro Man who had only to bend his finger to bring women running into his arms. Muscles yearned to be another Les Fuller, and often used his name as an alias to get women to like him.

Muscles was certainly not in the smuggling racket for the money because when he had it, he gave it away, mostly to women, often to strangers. He once bought a new Cadillac in Sherwood, Arkansas, and gave it to a woman he had met at the airport in Memphis, and only saw her once after that.

One of the members of the Cowboy Mafia told a story how Muscles pulled $20,000 out of his pocket and gave it to a woman he met at the Long Branch Saloon in Denton. This saloon was Muscles' favorite hangout that he called "his office" where he would proudly boast to women that he was a marijuana smuggler. Of course, no one ever believed him.

Willis Butler once told Larry Dale, "I hope Muscles doesn't give all the money away." "Those damn women play muscles."

He had been devastated by three wives who all ran out on him, taking every penny they could. Muscles may have known how to train horses, but women led him on a halter.

I really felt sorry for Muscles who wore custom Luchese boots, and had dime-store sunglasses hanging around his neck on a string. Granted he never intended to hurt Rex Cauble, who had been so good to him, but in the end that is exactly what happened.

Muscles never intended to hurt anyone. Muscles was taken advantage of my many a fast women.

*

John Ruppel's conviction was a shock because of my having known and liked the man for so long. He certainly didn't need to smuggle marijuana to make money. He was more than well-off, having made his fortune from the real estate boom in Pinellas County in Florida, as well as the machine-tool business he and his brother, a former County Commissioner, had established many years earlier.

He and his wife had retired to the Smoky Mountains in Sevierville, Tennessee, where they spent 3.5 million dollars on a four-level, forty-room mansion atop the Greystone Mountains overlooking Gatlinburg. Residents in the area took to calling his home "the castle" which became a big attraction for tourists. John himself was referred to as "the big man on the hill."

Muscles and I would often fly to Sevierville to take John boxes of prime steaks. Every time we walked in, John's face would light up like a kid at Christmas. He always enjoyed the simple, finer things in life. John struck me as a sincere, honest individual; which was why I could never understand how a man in his position could become involved in smuggling marijuana.

I remember one episode when Muscles and I arrived early due to a heavy tailwind that literally lifted and carried us from Denton to Tennessee at what felt like near warp speed. John and his wife were not due to get home for an hour or so, so we decided to grab a bite to eat at a local restaurant while we waited.

The young waitress was very friendly, and her good looks were not lost on Muscles, who stared goggle-eyed at her, as he did with any woman who came within six feet of him. The waitress asked if we were new in town. I told her we had flown in to bring John Ruppel some prime steaks from Texas.

"Oh, he'll love that," she gushed. "We don't get much prime beef in these parts."

She went on to expound on how respectable "the man on the hill" was, and how generous he was. She related how John had been approached for a donation toward building a recreational center for disadvantaged children. Instead of merely handing over a donation, he went ahead and paid for the entire center to be built.

Again, looking back, it was unfathomable to me that a man who cared so much for his community, who was so generous to those less fortunate, would risk losing everything and become involved in illegal dug smuggling.

John's generosity was well known. He gave $150,000 to build an Animal Shelter for Sevierville, and often bought pickup trucks for people who needed a car but couldn't afford to buy one. He had made his money and wasn't hesitant to share it with others less fortunate.

John was a trusting soul who took people at face value. He bought and paid for the Monkey, even put it in his own name, believing he was helping his friends Ray Hawkins and Muscles get into the shrimp business.

This was, of course, his big mistake, as it led to his being guilty by association like Rex was, and he was ultimately regarded as the one who financed the smuggling operation. It was clear to me that had he known what was really happening, he would never have put that boat in his own name. This was not consistent with someone intending to start smuggling marijuana.

Like Rex, John Ruppel paid the price for helping people. His life, his reputation and his fortune were sacrificed on the altar of David Baugh's ambition.

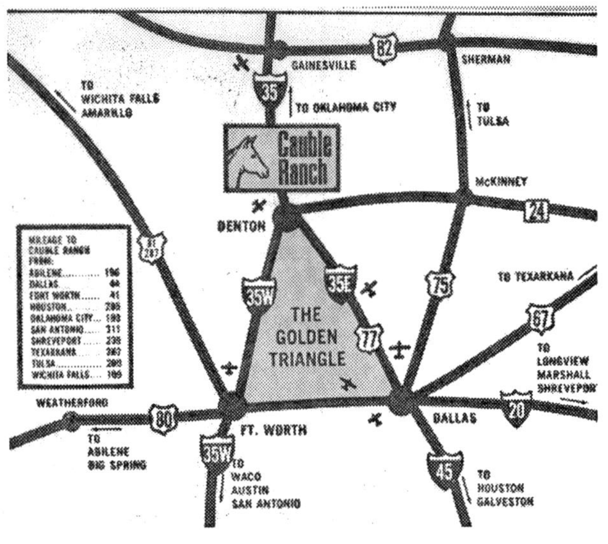
GAINESVILLE
82
SHERMAN
TO
WICHITA FALLS
AMARILLO
35
TO OKLAHOMA CITY
TO
TULSA
Cauble Ranch
McKINNEY
24
DENTON
287
MILEAGE TO
CAUBLE RANCH
FROM:
ABILENE.......... 196
DALLAS
FORT WORTH...... 41
HOUSTON
OKLAHOMA CITY
SAN ANTONIO..... 311
SHREVEPORT..... 238
TEXARKANA
TULSA
WICHITA FALLS.... 109
35W
35E
TO TEXARKANA
75
THE
GOLDEN
TRIANGLE
77
67
TO
LONGVIEW
MARSHALL
SHREVEPORT
WEATHERFORD
80
20
FT. WORTH
DALLAS
TO
ABILENE
BIG SPRING
35W
TO
WACO
AUSTIN
SAN ANTONIO
45
TO
HOUSTON
GALVESTON

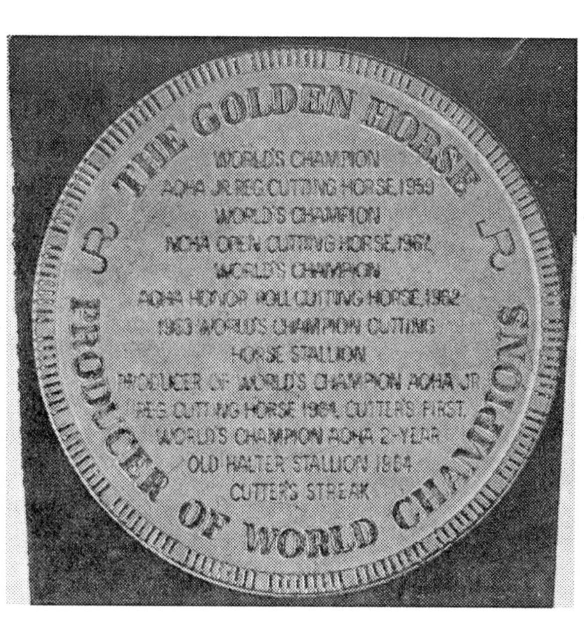
THE GOLDEN HORSE
WORLD'S CHAMPION
AQHA JR REG CUTTING HORSE 1959
WORLD'S CHAMPION
NCHA OPEN CUTTING HORSE 1962
WORLD'S CHAMPION
AQHA HONOR ROLL CUTTING HORSE 1962
1963 WORLD'S CHAMPION CUTTING
HORSE STALLION
PRODUCER OF WORLD'S CHAMPION AQHA JR
REG CUTTING HORSE 1964, CUTTER'S FIRST,
WORLD'S CHAMPION AQHA 2-YEAR
OLD HALTER STALLION 1964
CUTTER'S STREAK
PRODUCER OF WORLD CHAMPIONS

The greatest horse that ever looked through a bridle

Cowboy
Cessna Citation

COUNTY OF DALLAS §

On this the 30th day of April, 1984, Melvyn Carson Bruder personally appeared before me and, after being by me duly sworn, on his oath deposed and stated as follows:

"On April 27, 1984, I met and spoke with Lowell T. Miller in Denton, Texas. Mr. Miller advised me that he knew Raymond Eugene Hawkins and had been a good friend of Raymond Hawkins. Mr. Miller related to me the facts which he set out in the affidavit attached hereto, and further advised me that Hawkins told both Miller and an FBI agent in Dallas (who Miller identified as Masterson) that to the best of Hawkins' knowledge Rex Cauble had nothing to do with and was not involved in any of Hawkins' drug smuggling activities. Mr. Miller further told me that Hawkins told him he (Hawkins) was going to have to lie at Mr. Cauble's trial about Mr. Cauble's involvement in Hawkins' smuggling activities in order to avoid being prosecuted upon several charges and to obtain the benefit of his agreement with the Government."

MELVYN CARSON BRUDER

SWORN AND SUBSCRIBED TO before me, the undersigned authority, on this the 30th day of April, 1984.

NOTARY PUBLIC in and for the State of Texas

My Commission Expires:

STATE OF TEXAS §
COUNTY OF COOKE §

My name is Lowell T. Miller. I am a resident of Cooke County, Texas.

In the autumn of 1981, I was president of the Valley View National Bank in Valley View, Texas. Shortly after lunch in late September or early October of 1981, Raymond Hawkins came to see me at the bank. Mr. Hawkins was a customer to whom the bank had loaned money in the past. He maintained an account at the bank. On this occasion, Mr. Hawkins said that he had just done something that he didn't feel too good about. I asked him what it was and he said that he had just left the government agents and they had forced him to agree to testify against Rex Cauble at Cauble's upcoming trial. I told Hawkins that I thought he was pretty much out of trouble because I had heard that he had won a reversal of his own conviction. Hawkins told me that the FBI agents had told him that if he did not testify against Rex Cauble that they, the government, would try him on three separate felony counts, one at a time. Hawkins also told me that they had said they would not prosecute his wife, Karen, if he agreed to testify against Cauble. Hawkins further told me that he had no choice except to do whatever the government told him he had to do inasmuch as he did not have any money left to pay for a new trial on his reversed conviction and certainly no money to stand trial on the three separate felony trials he said the government had threatened to hold if he did not testify against Rex Cauble. After Hawkins left, I was so shocked by what he had said that I went out of my office and told the cashier of the bank, Mrs. Mildred Napier, of what Hawkins had told me.

The facts contained in this statement are a true and accurate account of my meeting with Raymond Hawkins in late September or early October, 1981 in my office at the Valley View National Bank in Valley View, Texas.

Lowell T. Miller

Rex, Cutterbill & Lep

Longbranch Saloon,
Denton, TX

Where the Cowboys leased the tractor-trailers.
Dallas, Texas.

UNITED STATES
POST OFFICE
HIGH ISLAND TEXAS
77623

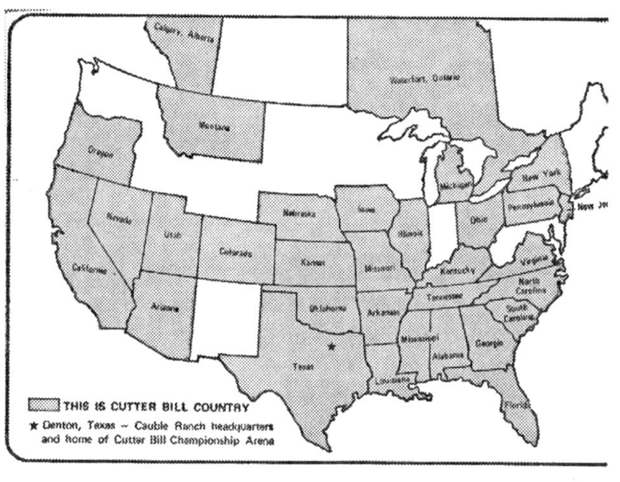

Calgary, Alberta
Montana
Oregon
Nevada
Utah
Colorado
California
Arizona
Nebraska
Kansas
Oklahoma
Texas
Iowa
Missouri
Arkansas
Louisiana
Mississippi
Alabama
Georgia
Florida
Tennessee
Kentucky
Ohio
Michigan
New York
Pennsylvania
Virginia
North Carolina
South Carolina
THIS IS CUTTER BILL COUNTRY
★ Denton, Texas – Cauble Ranch headquarters
and home of Cutter Bill Championship Arena

HUNSAKER
TRUCK
LEASE RENT

Ranch house of Ray Hawkins, cherokee Ranch.
Valley View, TX

STATEMENT OF CHARLES TALKINGTON GIVEN AT THE U. S. ATTORNEY'S OFFICE IN BEAUMONT, TEXAS, ON SEPTEMBER 4 and 5, 1979, TO SPECIAL AGENTS MICHAEL GRIMES AND DANIEL H. WEDEMAN IN THE PRESENCE OF HIS ATTORNEY, GEORGE PRESTON, RELATIVE TO HIS INVOLVEMENT IN MARIJUANA SMUGGLING.

I met Charles E. Foster, known to me as "Muscles" about eighteen (18) years ago. Ever since I was riding and showing horses in Madill, Oklahoma.

Since then I worked for "Muscles" off and on, at sales cleaning and showing horses and would occasionally work for Mr. Cauble on his ranch trimming horse's feet and brushing them (this would have had to been after Mr. Cauble had built his show barn about 1963).

It was about May of 1977 that "Muscles" wanted me to learn how to drive a diesel truck because he was planning on getting in the shrimp business. So, he rented a truck and had Willis Butler make some empty runs to places such as Wichita Falls and Orange, Texas, so we could learn how to drive it. CT

During the empty runs, I made 3 or 4 trips to Sneed Ship Yard in Orange, Texas, and practiced parking in the yard near the water. A little later, "Muscles" asked me if I wanted to be paid $10,000.00 to unload a shrimp boat full of Marijuana and to drive it somewhere.

About 2 or 3 weeks later I drove a truck (that we had rented from Hunsacker Trucking) to Sneed Ship Yard. Willis had gotten another truck from Hunsacker and followed me to the same place.

Willis Butler and myself were met by a man named Sneed (Martin Marion Sneed, Sr.), Charles Foster, Tommy Wimberely, Jimmy Wimberely, Carlos Gerdes, Raymond Hawkins and Jamie Holland.

Late that evening, a boat called the "Monkey" arrived with a load of Marijuana. We loaded my truck first, but Willis drove it away. They then loaded the truck that Willis brought down which I drove to Cauble's L.R. Ranch in Meridian, Texas, where we parked my truck in the barn with Willis'.

Jamie Holland, Muscles Foster, Carlos Gerdes, Raymond Hawkins, met myself and Butler and subsequently unloaded the diesel trucks onto pickup trucks belonging to customers. Butler and myself took two loads of Marijuana in a gooseneck trailer to Jamie Holland in Newport, Tennessee. Jamie paid Willis and me $3,000.00 for the first trip and $2,000.00 for the second trip each.

About January of 1978, Muscles Foster and myself drove to Savannah, Georgia, to unload some more Marijuana. We drove to a motel across from a truck stop where we met Larry Washington and Willis Butler (who had brought two trucks), Carlos Gerdes, Tommy Wimberly and John Doe Male. CT

After about 2 days, Foster told me to come back to Texas. So, Tommy Wimberly and myself drove back in Muscles' Suburban truck. I did not ask any questions because Muscles told me "if you don't know nothing, you can't say nothing".

About a week later, Muscles Foster, Tommy Wimberly and myself met at Thompson's Seafood located at High Island, Texas. Wimberly and myself spent about 2 nights in a trailer house. Muscles had left to go somewhere. CT

The following night, a boat came into Thompson's Seafood loaded with Marijuana which was met by myself, Tommy Wimberly, Jamie Holland, Carlos Gerdes, a couple of John Doe Males, and Willis Butler and Larry Washington (who had brought down two diesel trucks). We all helped unload the boat onto the two trucks. Afterwards, I rode with Larry Washington in one truck and Butler took the other truck and we drove them to Cauble's Crockett Ranch.

After unloading half of one truck onto customers' pickup trucks, the rest of the Marijuana was driven to Cauble's T. E. Mercer Ranch by Butler and Washington. Muscles and I went along in another car.

After the truck was driven to the T. E. Mercer Ranch, Muscles, Butler and Washington left. That left myself and a man named Jimmy. He (Jimmy) left with the first pickup truck that I had loaded with Marijuana. I stayed at the T. E. Mercer Ranch and loaded pickup trucks with Marijuana until the diesel truck was completely unloaded.

Afterwards, I swept out the truck and left the sweepings in a box which I thought I had put in the last customer's truck, but, he must have set it out because I heard later that Texas Rangers found it on the T. E. Mercer Ranch. I think that Jimmy might have owned part of this load because he had paid me $2,000.00 and had told me that he (Jimmy) had given $3,000.00 to Muscles Foster to be given to me later. So after unloading the last truck and returning it to Hunsacker Trucking (where Muscles ~~was waiting for me~~ [picked me CT]), he asked me how much money I had made. I told him and Muscles that he needed to borrow the $2,000.00 that Jimmy had given me. So I gave it to him. ~~(Muscles owed me $5,000.00).~~

After Muscles had picked me up, he drove me to the Crockett Ranch where Willis Butler and Larry Washington had taken the other truck. When we got there, the truck was almost completely unloaded. So, Muscles drove me to Madisonville, Texas, where we picked up the last customer's truck, took it to the Crockett Ranch, loaded it with Marijuana and returned it to the same place in Madisonville, Texas.

About April of 1978, Muscles Foster told me that he would pay me $10,000.00 to help unload another boat of Marijuana. Several days later, Muscles drove me to Thompson's Seafood at High Island, Texas. I was met there by Tommy Wimberly.

Both Wimberly and myself stayed in the trailer house there until the boat came in about a day later. It was met by myself, Carlos Gerdes, Tommy Wimberly, Jamie Holland. Willis Butler and Larry Washington were there because they had brought down two diesel trucks.

We unloaded the Marijuana off of the boat onto the two diesel trucks and took them to the Crockett Ranch where we again loaded the Marijuana onto customers' pickup trucks.

In conclusion, I would like to say that I was supposed to have been paid $10,000.00 by Muscles Foster for each of the three smuggling loads which I was involved in. That would total $30,000.00 which he owed me in addition to the $5,000.00 that was supposed to be paid me by Jimmy.

During my involvement with Muscles Foster, I have only hauled one load of shrimp. That was from Port Bolivar Fisheries in Port Bolivar, Texas, to Cauble's Denton Ranch where we tried to sell part of the shrimp. The remainder we took to Louisiana and tried to sell. Part of it we had to leave because it had gone bad.

The offload at High Island, TX

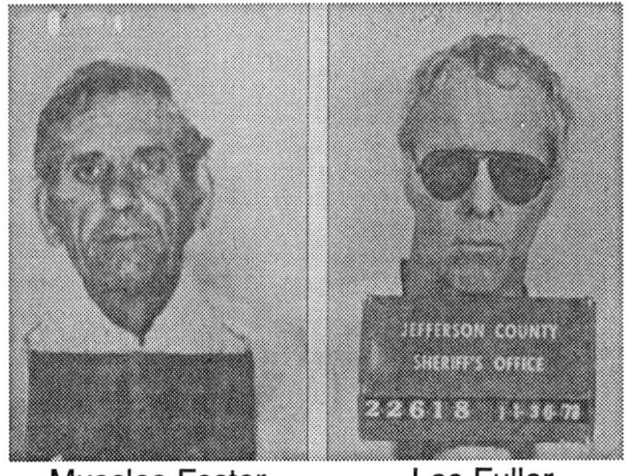

Muscles Foster Les Fuller

Thompson Seafood, High Island, TX. Notice the 18ft. entrance for the tractor-trailers

(Lt. to Rt.) John Connally, "Cutterbill," Rex Cauble

"The Aggie", the one that got away.

The Columbian Red Bud cargo. 40 pound bales.
High Island, TX.

Muscles office, formerly the Longbranch Saloon.

Ronald Regan, Lorne Green, Rex Cauble at LaCielo trail Ride. North California.

John & Nellie Connally at Rexs' trial. Tyler, TX.

Flying Presidential candidate John Connally and Campaign manager to Fund raiser. San Francisco, CA.

CHAPTER 9

Of course, during and after the trial of Muscles and his cowboy cohorts, details of their operation became known, and I was totally amazed that these men were able to pull off what they did.

Muscles was crazy, but as the saying goes, crazy like a fox. There were some things he was able to handle, many he couldn't. Perhaps it was really his associates who actually planned the operation, particularly

Carlos Gerdes, who was anything but ignorant. He was a highly educated man who knew his way around, no matter what social or business circle he might be in. The fact that he had kept the marijuana smuggling operation going for so long without being caught underscored his intelligent planning and flawless control over everything and everyone.

After Florida became too risky after the authorities cracked down, Carlos and Ray Hawkins looked elsewhere, and with Muscles' coming into the picture, they realized here was a golden opportunity to continue the smuggling in Texas. There was a coastline with many suitable harbors to unload the marijuana, after which it could then be transported by truck for ultimate distribution to dealers; and those places included some of Rex Cauble's ranches that Muscles had pinpointed as ideal for their needs.

After Texas became the focal point of their operation, four eight-five foot shrimp trawlers were used to bring the marijuana from Columbia. The boats cost between $200,000 and $250,000, and were equipped with saddle tanks to make the nine-day journey. These vessels, including the *Monkey*, the *Jubilee*, the *Bayou Blues* and the *Agnes Pauline*, were customized at Sneed's Shipyard in Orange, the largest vessel customizing facility in the Southwest owned by Martin Sneed, a veteran businessman in that part of Texas.

Prior to the trial of the cowboys, the sleepy little gulf town of Orange was only famous for having produced a first-round draft pick of the Dallas Cowboys - Cornerback Kevin "Pup" Smith at Texas A & M. While a football player at TCU, my son, J.R., played against Kevin.

Ray Hawkins, whom everyone called "Raymon", had paid Martin Sneed $250,000 for the use of his facilities, as well as for high security fences that were built so the boats could be unloaded without anyone observing the operation. Sneed got his sons involved in unloading the marijuana after one trip.

As a precaution against any attack, the boats were heavily armed with M-16's and various other weaponry. Carlos Gerdes was concerned over what he called "bandits" that were known to roam Columbian waters like the pirates of old. The boats were also rigged with plastic explosive so they could be blown up in the event of being apprehended by authorities. If this were to happen, the crew planned to escape using the scuba gear.

I felt this somewhat foolish because none of the cowboys were certified for scuba diving in open water. At the trial, Carlos testified that it was no secret in Columbia and Santa Marta that his shrimp boats were not risking hazardous travel on the high seas, often enduring monsoon-force winds, simply to transport boatloads of shrimp. They carried large sums of cash and loads of what David Baugh described as "high grade Colombian red bud marijuana."

Listening to all the statements made at the trial, I often marveled at the resourcefulness of these simple cowboys, or their foolish courage in order to rake in millions. In Carlos' statements, he revealed that they would unscrew the bottom of empty scuba tanks and hide the money inside, which I felt was a remarkably clever idea. They had to take hard cash, as their sources in Colombia demanded cash on delivery.

One load was carried on the "Jubilee" and after successfully crossing the stormy Atlantic, they would contact the supplier by radio, using the pre-arranged code words "Seabird to Dolphin" to identify themselves.

The first run out of Texas in the *Monkey* was a dry run. The ship arrived at Santa Marta and waited for several hours for their supplier to show. Finally the supplier radioed that the load would not arrive for several days, and instructed the smugglers to sail down the coast to Aruba and wait.

Understandably the cowboys were nervous over taking the ship down the Colombian coast without a legitimate reason, so they returned to Texas and docked back at High Island.

A month later they left for Colombia again, carrying, as they always did, 40,000 pounds of ice to preserve their perishables on the 18 day journey, as well as to create the illusion that they were legitimate shrimpers. But they never brought back any shrimp. Instead the boats were packed with 40,000 pounds of premium grade marijuana.

Carlos described how on one trip they anchored off the beach at Santa Marta and took a dinghy to shore to meet their contacts, after which they would return to the shrimp boat, stuff one million dollars in cash into pillow cases then return to shore to conclude the transaction. Once the money was handed over, Indians would load the marijuana into the boat.

Several Government witnesses detailed the operation, and one cowboy disclosed that prior to the third trip, he received nautical charts and instructions from Muscles. As I listened to the testimony, I remember thinking that was rather frightening considering Muscles' total lack of seagoing experience.

There was only one of the cowboys who had some background in sailing - Robert Hamm, of Tampa, Florida. It was his responsibility to find and give his opinion on the shrimpers before they were purchased. He was also responsible for overseeing the installation of radio equipment and the saddle fuel tanks.

Hamm was a horse farm employee of Ray Hawkins at the Madison Horse Farm, as well as the horse farm in Boston,

Georgia. He disclosed the fact that he was a crewman on the *Monkey* on their second trip to Colombia when they returned with a load of marijuana. Hamm related how, on their arrival back at High Island, Muscles came out to meet them and accompanied them into shore where he had constructed high security fences and had also dredged out the off-load spot next to the Thompson Seafood facility. This offload site was invisible from the inter coastal bridge. The Thompson seafood building had 18ft. high entrances on either side to enable the tractor-trailers to enter. 40,000 pounds could be offloaded in about 3 hours.

On that trip, the crew consisted of Ray Hawkins; Les Fuller; Charles Talkington, who was Muscles' black-smith; Willis Judge Butler, a child-hood friend of Muscles; Carlos Gerdes; and James Holland, a horse-breeding friend of Ray Hawkins. Also on board were two prostitutes, obviously along for the ride and the gratification of the crew.

Of course, these individuals were all actively involved in the physical side of the operation - guiding the boats to and from Colombia, picking up their illegal cargo, bringing it back and arranging distribution; but another of the kingpins was a distinct contrast to these physical types. He was a refined, decent-looking gentleman that most people would never have dreamed to be involved in smuggling marijuana but then, that was the image that John Ruppel conveyed by his appearance, his behavior and his manner. After meeting him, I regarded him as a wonderful old man. I especially admired him because he had made his fortune from scratch, something I always admire in a wealthy man.
He was an old friend of Ray Hawkins back in their Florida days.

He started out as a blue-collar worker in the machine tool business, but moved on to wind up making a small fortune by the time he was seventy years old. He owned a massive mansion in Sevierville, Tennessee. He had dabbled in horses, a common interest he had with Ray Hawkins, the consummate horse man in Florida.

It always puzzled me how Ray and Muscles talked him into investing in the shrimp boats. Obviously he felt that as Ray had made a fortune in the horse business, he would be equally successful starting up a shrimping business. Certainly John Ruppel had no interest in conspiring to smuggle drugs into the country. After all, he had sold out his business interests, retired and was living a very comfortable life in his four story mansion in the Smoky Mountains. The locals referred to him as "the man on the hill."

On several occasions I would fly Muscles to Tennessee with a couple of boxes of prime steaks for John Ruppel. This kind, trusting old man was as taken in by the fast-talking cowboys, just as Rex Cauble was. They trusted the cowboys, whom they regarded as "good ol' boys" and both lost out eventually, though John Ruppel did not lose as much of his fortune as Rex ultimately did.

I remember John Ruppel accompanying Muscles, Robert Hamm and Ray Hawkins to meet with Buddy Galfour in Port Aransas, Texas. Mr. Galfour was a boat broker. As an example of John Ruppel's naivete, he put the boats in his name. Certainly anyone planning a criminal enterprise would not be present while purchasing the shrimp boats, nor would they put their names down as owners, nor discuss with the boat broker the advantages and disadvantages of a freezer boat. But John Ruppel was obviously convinced that Muscles and Ray were serious about going into the shrimp business.

The fact that Ruppel became involved only underscores the fact that he was ignorant of the pending drug smuggling operation that Muscles and Ray Hawkins were planning. In fact, the only actual evidence against John Ruppel was the fact that two of the shrimp boats were in his name, plus the testimony of a few scared cowboys that were coerced into a plea bargain to clear themselves or possibly achieve lenient sentences.

It is truly scary that what happened to Rex and John Ruppel could have happened to anyone. At both trials the prosecution took all the evidence and maintained that anyone who came in contact with the cowboy smugglers were presumed guilty. In other words, guilt by association. The jury disregarded the customary instructions to maintain a presumption of innocence until proven guilty, and not to turn in a guilty verdict if there were any reasonable doubts remaining. But this did not happen.

Both Rex and John Ruppel had attachable assets, which was the government's motive. If these men were convicted, the government would profit handsomely.

In contrast to these two rich, successful, educated men, the majority of the Cowboy Mafia were working cowboys. The leader, Carlos Gerdes, was the brains behind the operation, the one who did all the planning, plus he had all the contacts in Bogota and Santa Marta in Colombia.

Carlos pleaded guilty to all ten counts, was fined $150,000 and given twenty years in Federal prison with no parole. At the time he was convicted, Carlos had an eight month old son at home.

I would like to say that if young Christopher Gerdes reads this story about his father, I must state that Carlos was a man with more courage than anyone I have ever known. He faced the music and took his punishment like a man. He would not give in to government pressure and would not rat on the two men - Rex Cauble and John Ruppel – that he knew were innocent.

I shall never forget at the trial, when the relentlessly ego-driven David Baugh read out the list of ten indictments, Carlos responded quite calmly to each count: "Guilty." David Baugh glared at him.

"Are you crazy?" he demanded. Carlos replied again. "Guilty, your Honor."

Yes, Carlos Gerdes was quite a man, one of many involved in the Cowboy Mafia that I shall never forget.

*

Among all the memories I have of the Cowboy Mafia, my sympathies still linger most for John Ruppel, a man who was totally honest and forthright. Maybe he was naive, and if he was, he paid the penalty for not being as sharp as he should have been. He picked the wrong company and was guilty by association, nothing more.

The hand-picked jury in Tyler, Texas, was a real "Robin Hood" jury. Ruppel had been found guilty on four counts of a seven-count indictment. After three trials he was sentenced and fined. He got a five year sentence, convicted of "conspiracy." Which was ridiculous to me. He had no part in any conspiracy. He merely associated with Ray Hawkins and Muscles Foster.

As John stated in his trial, he had been deceived by two men who talked him into helping them finance a shrimp boat, and transact the purchase of another. Both these vessels were used for smuggling marijuana, but Ruppel had been under the impression they were to be used to start a shrimping business.

He had no part in the smuggling operation whatsoever. He never even knew about it until twelve defendants were arrested after the Agnes Pauline pulled into port to be met by the authorities. Before this, John Ruppel never knew what was going on.

After two and a half hours on the stand, John Ruppel told of requests by Muscles that resulted in the purchase of the *Monkey*, a boat that was involved in several shipments of marijuana from Colombia to Texas.

Ruppel also testified that he handled transactions involving the transfer of ownership of the *Jubilee*, handling the money and documents for the vessels, which was true. He also described a series of meetings with Muscles and Ray Hawkins, meetings at which he thought they were to discuss their shrimping business. He met at the Marina Hotel at the DFW Airport to discuss the possibility of selling the *Monkey* to Muscles, who turned out to be only interested in leasing it. Muscles did not want the boat in his name, which was just another example of the devious dealings he had with John Ruppel that led to the downfall of a wonderful man.

CHAPTER 10

Looking back today on those tumultuous events, many details surface in my mind., especially in regard to Muscles Foster.

When Ray Hawkins decided to move to Denton, Muscles felt inclined to help him get acquainted and settle into his new surroundings. He told Ray that the Cherokee Ranch was for sale, and Ray went ahead and bought it.

Many mornings when I was doing my daily check on Muscles for Rex, I would find Muscles up at the Cherokee

Ranch. Ray had started a massive redecoration, including a massive horse barn with several stalls and an area for the general care of the horses. The barn was so large it can be seen from the highway, and overshadowed the rather modest house in front. It became clear that Ray was serious about his horse business. He had made a lot of money breeding and trading horses in Florida and in Georgia.

After Ray moved to the Cherokee Ranch, Ron Smith, one of his employees from the Madison, Florida ranch moved to Denton and began working for Muscles. Ron Smith had met Ray some years earlier in the Appalachian Correction Facility.

Ron Smith had been incarcerated for possession of stolen property; Ray had been arrested and imprisoned following a seizure of 37 tons of marijuana. Roy Smith tried to get his parole moved to Georgia so he could be close to the Boston Horse Farm where he went to work for Ray. His request was denied and he was paroled to Panama City on December 31, 1976. Ray told him to take a bus to Thomasville, Georgia and call him at the Boston Hose Farm. Once he arrived, Ray asked if he could drive a tractor-trailer truck, and he was hired.

On one occasion he had to take a load from Quitman, Georgia to Jamie Holland's ranch in Newport, Tennessee. Ron had trouble driving the big unit and ran into a ditch. Using a two-way radio, Ron called for help, and Muscles and Ray Hawkins arrived to rescue him. They called a tow truck and paid the driver $2,000 in cash to pull the trailer-tractor out of the ditch.

While they waited for the tow truck, Ray was robbed at gunpoint of $67,000 in cash. Ron Smith testified later that after this episode, Ray was always nervous about carrying large sums of cash.

They hid the trailer in a field and

returned to the Boston Horse Farm, picked up another truck and went back to pick up the trailer. When they got back, they unloaded eight tons of marijuana into the barn. The other half of the load was distributed from the field.

When he moved to Texas, Ron Smith was thirty years old, about the same age as two of his eventual partners in the smuggling operation, Larry Dale Washington and Charles Talkington.

Muscles told me he truly welcomed Ron Smith's move to Denton. Being the lonely man he was, he now had someone to run around with. Before Ron came on the scene, he had few buddies.

In fact, Muscles' previous brushes with the law were perhaps one of the many reasons for his lack of close friends as well as his fragile mental and emotional state.

In the early 70's he had helped several other cowboys offload a load of marijuana, for which he was paid $10,000 and one pound of grass. Later he and the cowboys were arrested and one of the cowboys later testified that they were taken by DEA agents to a hotel room out of town, questioned and beaten. They subsequently filed charges against the agents, but the charges were dropped the next day. When the operation moved to Texas, the chain of command included Ray Hawkins and Carlos Gerdes, who put up the money. These two, together with Muscles, would bring the money to the boat together with maps and charts. Muscles would determine where the marijuana was to be offloaded after he cleared the ranch to make sure no one would be there to witness the operation. Pickup trucks with campers were left with the keys in the ignition. These trucks had license plates from all over the country. The trucks would be loaded with about 1,500 pounds of marijuana and returned to where they came from and again left with keys in the ignition so the distributors could drive them off to the dealers. Ray Hawkins and Carlos Gerdes often bought a percentage of the load and deal themselves.

The rest of the load would be loaded into gooseneck trailers that Larry Dale and Willis Judge would drive to Jamie Holland's ranch in Newport, Tennessee, or to the Boston farm from which the grass would be distributed. Payment from the dealers was delivered to the airport where Hawkins or Gerdes would collect it and take it back to the ranch. After the money arrived, the cowboys would be paid their share.

On one occasion Larry Dale Washington and Willis Judge Butler were driving a load from the Crockett Ranch in Texas to Newport, Tennessee, when they were stopped by the DPS for not having mud flaps on the tractor-trailer.

I can imagine how nervous they must have been, knowing what was inside the trailer. They had covered the marijuana with alfalfa hay, but there had always been the possibility that the smell would alert the officers; but all the two smugglers got was a citation for the mud flap violation, and they continued on their way.

Many afternoons Muscles and Larry Dale would drop by our house and have a cold beer. One afternoon just prior to the trial, Larry Dale stopped by on his own, which surprised me. He usually had Muscles with him on these visits. But later, it came out at the trial that Agent Grimes and DEA Agent Masterson had put Larry up to it, and had rigged him with a body mike. This was obviously a vain attempt by the authorities to get some evidence against Rex because they had nothing on Rex that would have supported an indictment.

Larry Dale also traveled to Sevierville, Tennessee, wearing a body mike in the vain hope of recording some evidence from John Ruppel. But he and Agent Masterson could never find the Ruppel mansion, which only underscored my impression of them both. Like most of the cowboys whose greed got them involved in the smuggling operation, they were not very bright. Together they may have had an IQ of 100…

Jamie Holland had met Muscles at the Boston Horse farm. Muscles told Ray later that he felt Jamie Holland would be a good mule, unloading the grass off the boats. Just like Muscles, Jamie soon tired of the back-breaking work and wanted to become more deeply involved. This led to Jamie's farm in Newport, Tennessee becoming another drop off point.

*

At Rex's trial, Larry Dale was extremely nervous. Like all the cowboys, he had plea bargained and had been briefed by the authorities on how to respond. It was no wonder they were all so nervous and had to be told to relax several times. In contrast, I was not the least nervous on the stand when I was called to the stand. I knew they had nothing on Rex other than what they might coerce out of the handful of scared, programmed cowboys who would say anything to lessen the penalties for their involvement.

As Rex's trial progressed, it became clear to me that the cowboys were not the only ones with minimal intelligence. The jury was no better. Rex was certainly not being tried by a jury of his peers. I regarded them a bunch of wood tick jurors, certainly not blue collar types, and they were obviously influenced by the massive media coverage of the trial. TIME magazine was there, NEWSWEEK was there, plus dozens of others eager to glean as much of the sensational case as they could.

The jury was doubtless impressed by the ongoing media circus. On two occasions Judge William Steger had to reprimand jurors for discussing the case with the media, and eventually let two jurors go for speaking with reporters.

I still feel that if the case had been moved to a different venue, the outcome would have been different. Understandably, the jury was impressed with Rex's wealth, and presumed that anyone with so much accumulated wealth must have made it illegally. Which was certainly not the case.

Members of the jury were all minimum wage-earners, and I know from my personal experience that the have-nots are always envious of those who have it all. Plus, those who have it seldom mix with those who don't. So Rex was at a disadvantage in having his fate decided by individuals who would only regard him with distrust and envy.

But Rex was no social snob. Early in life he learned to treat people with respect regardless of their financial position. Perhaps as things turned out, it had not been wise for him to be so friendly with the cowboys who eventually cost him everything he had ever worked for. They took advantage of his kindness and his generosity.

In contrast to the cowboys' testimony on the stand, I spoke the truth and nothing but the truth: that Rex Cauble was innocent, and had no idea what these cowboys were doing on his ranches. Nobody had any idea except the cowboys themselves, and it was easy for them to conceal their operation on Rex's four thousand acre ranches.

I said it then, and I'll say it again: Rex Cauble was an honorable man with integrity who would never have done anything as dangerous as smuggling marijuana. He was a stickler for honesty as I discovered many times in his dealings with people.

I recall one episode at the Meacham Airport in Fort Worth, Texas, where we hangared Rex's airplane. We had been overcharged by about twenty-five hundred dollars. I was aware of this because I personally signed all the fuel bills.

I reported the matter to Rex.

"I don't believe it," he gasped in amazement. "We've been such good customers. They wouldn't do that, surely."

Rex contacted the airport, trying to straighten out the incorrect charge, but got nowhere. They locked the doors and would not pull the airplane out of the hangar. Obviously they were trying to take advantage of a man whose wealth was legendary.

A few days later Rex came by to talk.

"Roy, I hate to say it, but these folks are trying to rip me off," he said regretfully. "Let's move our business to Denton airport."

One night my son, J.R. accompanied me to Meacham Field, in Fort Worth, and we fired up the turboprops in the hangar. The two big 650 horse power engines were so powerful, I thought they might blow the hangar down. It shook like there was a tornado outside. We got the plane out, and proceeded to fly it to Denton airport. We never again did business with Meacham Airport.

*

Back to Muscles and Ron Smith:

Often Muscles would drop by the house for dinner, and I was always friendly and courteous, as I felt sorry for the man. He was always trying to impress people in order to be liked; or so he thought.

Ron Smith lived in a house up on Mexican Hill, and was kept busy with the renovations to the Cherokee Ranch. When the cowboys trial came down the pike, Ron testified for the government because like all the cowboys, he was scared by David Baugh, who made them say whatever was needed to build a case against Rex.

One afternoon I was sitting in

Rex's office on University Road in Denton, when a truck pulled up with Ray and Ron inside. Ray got out, walked into the office, and told Rex he wanted to buy a horse that Muscles had recommended. I remember wondering why Ron hadn't come in with Ray, but later in court, he testified that Ray had instructed him to stay in the pickup because they had a bale of marijuana stashed in the cab.

At the trial, I remember Ron was extremely nervous on the stand while he was being questioned, so much so that the prosecutor finally told him to relax. Ron testified that he had transported Ray's horses from the Boston Horse Farm in Georgia to the Cherokee. He claimed Ray said he was moving to Texas because there were fewer checkpoints at which their smuggling operation might have been discovered. "Wide open space, in Texas," Ron testified.

Ray was a net horse buyer of horses in Denton and Wichita Falls.

Back in Georgia, Ray would stash large sums of cash at his attorney's office in Quitman, Georgia because, as Ron told the court, Ray was always nervous about carrying large sums of cash with him. After he moved to the Cherokee Ranch, he would bury large sums of money in the horse stalls. And he had plenty. He spent over $300,000 on improvements to the ranch.

He hired all the young cowboys to work on the improvements, including constructing fences and new buildings. He paid them daily in hundred dollar bills. The cowboys were grossly over paid, and spent most of their money down at the Long Branch saloon in Denton, which was Muscles' favorite hangout.

One night Muscles and Larry Dale drove back drunk, and ran their old Camino through the barbed wire fence and took out a couple of fence poles in the process. Muscles called me to come and rescue them, and when I arrived, they cold barely stand. Larry

Dale was swaying back and forth with a large bulge in his cheek. He had almost a can of Copenhagen in his mouth.

"Doesn't that stuff make you sick?" I asked.

"Nah, man, I sleep with a dip in my mouth," was his slurred response.

Muscles always liked to go drinking with the younger cowboys, hoping that they could corral some female company. But the cowboys told me the minute Muscles started talking with a woman, she would turn away in disgust.

Once at the bar, I heard him tell again, for probably the thousandth time, that he was a drug smuggler, hoping to impress the attractive young woman sitting beside him at the bar.

The female bartender laughed contemptuously.

"Muscles, get some new material," she told him.

No one believed him, and no one ever took him seriously

Muscles Foster smuggles drugs? *No way.*

But Ray Hawkins was a far cry from Muscles. He was quiet about business and wealthy, smart and intelligent. Ron related that when he brought the horses from Quitman, he was told to bring a large briefcase filled with money with him. The briefcase held over $200,000 in cash.

When this came out in court, I remember thinking that Ray must have trusted Ron Smith implicitly to carry this out. Ray himself said later that he had to trust someone besides his wife, Karen, who had secured lock boxes all over the place for their cash funds.

At the trial, Karen was in the clear, and was not even arrested because of the plea bargain that Ray had with the government. This was a surprise, because she could just as easily been charged with criminal knowledge, just as Jamie Hollands' wife had been.

But the deal the government made with the cowboys was too good to refuse. And the cowboys were quite a bunch.

I remember once I flew a party of them down to Houston to go bird hunting. Larry Dale, Willis Judge, Charles all talked up a storm on the flight down from Denton. We all stayed at Rex's apartment on Westheimer, which was leased by Cutter Bills to accommodate any out of town customers who flew in to buy the expensive Western clothing.

The next morning Muscles asked if I would run down to Oshmans and pick up some shells.

"Get about 50 boxes," I was told.

Which made sense to me. They would need a lot of ammunition because none of them could hit the side of a barn at fifty feet.

At the trial, it was revealed

that they never wanted those shells for bird hunting. They were intended for the *Bayou Blues*, part of Muscles' idea to arm the boats with weapons and plastic explosives in order to blow up the boat and destroy evidence if they were ever stopped by the authorities.

When I heard this, I chuckled at the thought. The only thing they would have blown up would have been themselves. None of the cowboys had ever been at sea, not even out on a fresh water lake, yet here they were planning to take a small shrimp boat hundreds of miles across the Atlantic Ocean to Colombia. Muscles himself confessed this to me once when I asked him if he wanted to go fishing with me out on Lake Lewisville.

"Shit, man," he replied. "I ain't never been fishing. I spent all my life messing with horses on ranches."

Les Fuller had never been boating, either, yet he was Captain of the ship when they all took off for Colombia on a trip. Les was a drug-store cowboy, dressed to the nines in all the fancy duds from Rex's Cutter Bills stores in Dallas and Houston.

Les Fuller a real cowboy? *No way...*

Only the others like Ron Smith, Larry Dale, Willis Judge and Charles were real cowboys who knew what to do around a ranch and how to handle horses.

CHAPTER 11

As my mind drifts back over the years, I remember details of so many people who were connected with the Cowboy Mafia. I have concluded that the driving force among ostensibly honest, hard-working individuals was the irresistible temptation to make a pile of easy money quickly despite the possible dangers involved.

This is probably what led to the downfall of Martin Sneed and his family after they become involved. I met Martin several times on the trips down the Gulf Coast when Muscles was supposedly getting into the shrimp business. Martin Sneed, Senior, was a very successful shipyard owner in Orange, Texas. Helping him in his business were his two sons, Martin, Jr., and Clyde. Martin must have been in his late 50's, and the two brothers around 30. Their large coastal shipyard was the typical multi-generational family-owned and operated business that enjoyed a major share of the market for shrimp boat customization and maintenance.

On one trip I flew Ray Hawkins and Muscles to Orange to meet with Martin Sneed and discuss the acquisition of a shrimp trawler. As Ray boarded the N3063W aircraft, I noticed he was carrying a large stainless steel briefcase. Muscles told me later that it contained money to pay for a shrimp boat. I never asked any questions. I was there merely to fly the aircraft; though I will never deny that many times my curiosity was aroused by the back-and-forth conversations of the men seated behind me in the plane.

We met Martin Sneed at a local seafood restaurant in Orange. They talked at great length about shrimp boats and the local market. As it turned out, the money in that stainless steel briefcase was not to buy a boat, but rather a payoff to entice Martin Sneed into becoming involved in the smuggling operation Muscles was setting up in Texas. Obviously Mr. Sneed was drawn in by the prospect of quick and easy money, and understandably so. Ray Hawkins paid him $150,000 in cash for the use of his facilities as well as having his two sons help unload the boats. Martin, Jr,. and Clyde were paid $10,000 each for becoming two of the "mules" that unloaded the marijuana. They also received several pounds of grass as additional compensation.

Sneed was to provide a safe offloading spot at his shipyard around which unusually tall fences would be constructed, together with other security measures.

He was given an additional $250,000 to purchase a suitable boat, which turned out to be the *Jubilee*, an 85 foot shrimp boat with 60,000 pound capacity. The vessel was outfitted with ship-to-shore radios, heavy artillery, extra fuel tanks for the long trip to Colombia, plus plastic explosives. This work was all done at Sneed's shipyard.

But like Muscles and Jamie Holland, the Sneed family soon succumbed to greed and wanted a bigger piece of the pie and became involved in distribution of the illegal cargo. They acted as lookouts for the boats as they arrived back from Colombia, and offloading was done alternately between the Sneed shipyard and High Island. They never offloaded at the same place and because of their familiarity with the coastline, they were able to make sure the "coast was clear" - even to diverting other boat traffic that might have impeded the unloading.

Mr. Barrow, the land owner at High Island, was also well paid above the market value of the property when Muscles established the "Thompson Seafood Company". It certainly seemed that all the locals had a vested interest in the cowboys smuggling operation because it meant more bucks in their pockets. They were all paid handsomely for their contributions, and always in cash.

The Sneed brothers eventually started distributing one to two thousand pounds themselves. Just before the *Agnes Pauline* was met by the authorities and the operation came to a screeching halt, Clyde Sneed was arrested after the DPS Narcotics Unit found 1,400 pounds of marijuana in his attic. The DEA served a warrant, searched the Sneed house in Orange and found thirty cardboard boxes labeled "Product of Colombia." Each box contained 40 pounds of Colombian red bud marijuana.

It truly amazed me that the Sneed family had become so involved with the smuggling. At their trial, Martin Senior literally had the book thrown at him and he was sentenced to six years in the Federal Correctional Facility. His two sons got two years in addition to large fines. Later, Martin Senior paid off a probation officer to lessen the probation period for Martin, Jr.

The government later bargained with Martin Senior to testify against the probation officer with the promise that this would help, not hurt him. *Wrong!* This was but another example of the unending shenanigans that characterized both the trial of the cowboys as well as the trial of Rex Cauble.

Judge William Steger, who at that time was the highest ranking judge in the Eighth District of Texas, was so incensed he wrote a sharp letter to the Correctional Facility lambasting their actions against Mr.

Sneed.

Remembering the many times I had visited Orange and talked with the Sneeds, I felt they were a hard-working diligent family that had been led astray by the possibility of making a quick buck. Again, their greed led to their downfall, just as happened eventually to all the members of the Cowboy Mafia.

*

It has always made me curious why and how the authorities start investigating any person for possible criminal activity. In the case of Martin Sneed, it seems things started happening only after local DEA agents found 1400 pounds of marijuana at the home of Clyde's cousin, Richard Sneed. Their suspicions aroused, they began an investigation which resulted in the Bayou Blues coming under their scrutiny. The vessel was listed at an address: 2011 Dupont Drive in Orange, which happened to be the address of Sneed's Shipyard.

Inspector Harrison went to Sneed's shipyard, introduced himself to Clyde as a customs inspector. Clyde was the shipyard foreman, and was always in charge, something Muscles and I noticed every time we happened to visit.

Clyde told the inspector that he was in charge of the shipyard as well as the *Bayou Blues*, the 85 foot shrimper that was docked there. Clyde said the boat was owned by his father, Martin Sneed, Sr., through MMS Leasing, Inc. The inspector demanded to see the registration documents.

Clyde stated that the records were filed at the shipyard office. Agent Harrison then boarded the Bayou Blues, something that legally required him to have a search warrant, which he did not have and for which there was no probable cause.

A short time thereafter, the Assistant District Attorney David Baugh met with Agent Gray who informed him of what was going on. There was constant arguing over who was going to handle an investigation. It had been the DPS that was responsible for the seizure of the 1400 pounds of marijuana in Richard Sneed's home. Understandably the DPS wanted to part of the operation, and argued with David Baugh over whose jurisdiction this would come under. They met with Lieutenant Green Moree at the Orange County Sheriff's office.

The Lieutenant claimed that as it was his office that seized the marijuana, they should have jurisdiction over the pending investigation. The bickering was endless, with everyone wanting to get in on the action.

The investigation began in September, 1977. Through surveillance and confidential informants information, it finally became clear that the Bayou Blues was being used to transport more than just shrimp.

Clyde had given Agent Harrison permission to board the Bayou Blues even though such an inspection was illegal without a search warrant. During his search, Harrison happened to find charts and maps of the coastal area around Sabine, Texas. The charts were marked with positions approximately 80 miles south of Sabine Pass. It came out later at the trial that this search was in complete violation of the law.

But whether the search was legal or not, enough evidence was unearthed to bring about charges and the eventual trial of Martin Sneed and his accomplices.

I will not debate the legal or moral aspects of smuggling marijuana, but whatever crime anyone may commit, investigations should be done within the confines of the law, and this was not done in the case of the *Bayou Blues*.

This is, to me, an example of the dubious ethics involved when the authorities decide to go after someone. They went after Martin Sneed and he paid the price for his illegal activities and the government came out ahead with all the money they confiscated under the Racketeer-Influenced and Corrupt Organizations Act.

This was also true in the case of Rex Cauble when the Treasury wound up richer by millions of dollars. Again, greed was the motivation for the prosecution rather than merely bringing criminals to justice.

If U.S. prosecutors did not have the luxury of the arcane laws of the Racketeer-Influenced and Corrupt Organizations Act, the outcome for Rex would have been a lot different. Ninety million dollars in attachable assets would not have been seized, nor would have U.S. Assistant Attorney David Baugh have had special funding from the Justice Department to fund the three year investigation.

After Baugh received this special funding, there was no turning back despite the fact that any and all evidence was purely circumstantial. According to Baugh's superior,

U.S. Attorney John Hannah, Baugh did not even have enough evidence to indict Rex, which was a strong point of contention between these two men. It was obvious that David Baugh's burgeoning law career was on the line.

*

Thinking back on the many cases dealing with major public figures where millions, sometimes billions of dollars have been involved, one often finds that such illegal operations have their beginning in board rooms of major corporations, and the guilty parties are frequently well-known individuals.

But those who ran the forty million dollar operation of the Cowboy Mafia were not slick-suited businessmen in an ivory tower in downtown Dallas. The whole smuggling operation was herded over by a bunch of Texas cowboys who would usually be found in a beer joint, swigging cold bottles of Lone Star beer, chain-smoking Camel cigarettes and listening to good ol' country music. And people like Muscles Foster, Ray Hawkins, Larry Dale Washington, Willis Judge Butler and their close associates were no small time crooks who got together to discuss possibly holding up a convenience store for a few bucks. Giving credit where credit is due, they successfully set up the largest marijuana smuggling activities in the history of Texas.

After the authorities stepped in and the details became public knowledge, I found it hard to believe that this bunch of not-overly-educated cowboys could have initiated such a mammoth enterprise. After all, they did not merely bring in a few loads of marijuana for their personal use and perhaps sell a bag or two to their friends.

They had every detail planned, down to the last detail. After they took the shrimp boats to Bogota, each vessel returned with a full load of prime Colombian red bud marijuana that was transported to various ranches belonging to their unsuspecting wealthy civic leader, Rex Cauble, and from there it was distributed to major dealers around the country. A two million dollar investment would mushroom into 35 million in street sales.

This was a major undertaking, and evolved into a classic case of guilt by association for Rex, who as a result became the focus of Assistant U.S. Attorney David Baugh, out to pin the blame on this man and confiscate his enormous fortune for which he had worked long and hard to achieve by honest means. Clearly, prosecutors can make a fair trial impossible, especially when so much is at stake.

I learned that the cowboys and close friends they recruited to join the smuggling operation usually met and formulated their plans in pastures on one of Rex's many ranches, or at the Long Branch Saloon in Denton or in bars along the Texas coast. After they completed their trip to Colombia and returned with the marijuana, they would get their share, stuff their boots with money and head for the nearest watering hole and spend their ill-gotten gains on liquor and women.

The media reported that each load on the shrimp boats was worth 30 million dollars. In actuality, it was more like 40 million. In the three years they operated, the cowboys made twelve trips to Colombia and hauled back marijuana worth over 300 million dollars.

It was incredible that they were able to do all this considering the caliber of men involved - plain good ol' cowboys eager to make more money than they ever could in their life-times of working on a ranch, training cutting horses.

For a long time whenever I would talk with veterinarians, horsemen and ranchers about Muscles Foster being the head honcho of the Cowboy Mafia, there were always hoots of laughter and total expressions of disbelief that this half-crazy middle-aged world champion horse trainer could have been so closely involved, and moreover, that Muscles had been able to keep things going as long as he did. However, Muscles did have loads of experience in the "Cowboy Mafia," notably Ray Hawkins and Carlos Gerdes from Madison and St. Petersburg, Florida, respectively. These cowboys had two decades of experience in marijuana smuggling. Ray Hawkins, Carlos Gerdes, Harry "The Hat" Hannon, and Muscles, were successful for several years operating out of Ray Hawkins' Madison, Florida, horse farm, St. Petersburg, and Tampa, Florida. It was at a watering hole in Madeira Beach, Florida, that Harry "The Hat" Hannon became acquainted with Harry Coursey, the undercover agent of the Georgia Bureau of Investigation, only by chance.

CHAPTER 12

The Cowboy Mafia trial was over, but sentencing of the prosecution witnesses was delayed until after the trial of Rex Cauble. This was part of the plea bargain agreement with the cowboys to insure they all cooperated in Rex's trial. The biggest marijuana smuggling operation had been closed down and as far as the public was concerned, that was the end of it.

But David Baugh did not let the matter rest. For over two years he had pursued a possible indictment of Rex Cauble, for whom he maintained an ongoing animosity. If ever there was an unrelenting, ego-driven individual eager to advance his career, it was David Baugh, who was out to get Rex Cauble and confiscate his millions for the government. He was the hatchet man determined to foster his own reputation by convicting this respected, wealthy Texas businessman for crimes he did not commit. Eventually Baugh's diatribe of hatred resulted in ongoing name-calling between them, and even Baugh's associates disagreed with his remarks, especially when there were no facts to back up the endless accusations.

Baugh's background illustrated of his lifelong obsession for elevating himself into the judicial stratosphere. While in college, he became a political activist. He wound up in Virginia where he sued the state to get his law degree and also achieved a reputation as a radical student. He kicked around upstate New York for a while as a social worker; then in

1972 he went to Houston, Texas, to pursue a legal career.

His past activities followed him, and he confessed humorously to a Beaumont newspaper that many regarded him "as a SDS (Students for a Democratic Society) lawyer with a bomb in one hand and Chairman Mao's little red book in the other."

He got a job as Federal Prosecutor in Beaumont, a position that resulted from U.S. Attorney John Hannah appointing him because, as he said, "he hired Baugh because it was his first opportunity to hire a black man to increase respect for the justice system among blacks."

So when David Baugh indicted Rex Cauble on August 7, 1981, waves of disbelief swept through everyone who knew him in the State of Texas.
Rex was indicted on ten counts of violations of the Federal Racketeer-influenced and Corrupt organizations Act.

He had intended using G.

Brockett Irwin as his attorney, but fate decreed otherwise. A few weeks after the cowboys' trial ended, Mr. Irwin happened to go sailing on Lake Tyler. He was sailing across the water and his sailboat passed beneath a high voltage wire over the lake. Irwin was leaning against the mast at the time. In a flash, the current went to ground through the mast and Irwin was electrocuted. So instead of Irwin, Rex hired Jack Gray, together with Roy Minton, as the two men to defend him against the outrageous charges leveled against him.

A warrant was issued and handed to the Deputy Marshall in Tyler, Texas. Rex's bond appearance was sent at $250,000 by U.S. Magistrate Roger Sanders. This was preposterous and totally shocking. Newspapers including the Dallas Morning News used the word "superficial" to describe the indictments.

On August 27 Rex traveled to Sherman, Texas, with his legal counsel to post bond, after which he was released.

"I am innocent, and I will be vindicated in court," Rex stated afterwards.

Three counts accused Rex of racketeering. Each carried a maximum penalty of 20 years in prison and a fine of only $25,000.

It was clear to me and everyone else that David Baugh and the prosecution had set their sights on more than $25,000. Why not a million, I wondered? As it turned out, they got many millions...

The first count alleged that Rex had conspired to carry out racketeering activity affecting interstate and foreign trade. He was accused of conspiring to smuggle 250,000 pounds of high grade marijuana from Colombia to the Texas cities of High Island, Port Arthur and Orange as well as being accused of conspiring with others in the smuggling operation.

The forty page indictment also

alleged that Rex had embezzled $147,000 from the Western State Bank in Denton. Rex owned 51% of these banks, which made these claims preposterous. At the time, Rex was worth more than 100 million. He would certainly not risk embezzling a mere $147,000 from his own bank. That was "chump change" to him...

On one of our many talks together, Rex said he welcomed the trial in order to clear his name, and everyone who knew him agreed that he would be acquitted. Like everyone who knew Rex would agree, the Honorable eight-term Federal State District Judge Byron Matthews stated later that he thought Rex Cauble had been framed. He appeared as a character witness at the trial. Many people felt that Rex had become a victim of selective prosecution.

Judge Matthews' statement was not speculation. He was a most respected judge in Tarrant Count, and had known Rex for over thirty years.

At the Judge's request, he was interviewed by Special Agents Joseph Masterson and John W. Strickland, Jr.. He told them he had been a judge for over eighteen years. He was elected, not appointed, and each period ran for four years. He told the special agents that Rex had not seen many of his ranches for over twelve years. He was too busy with other business matters.

Judge Matthews was a most credible witness. Although he and Rex had been involved in the horse business and he knew Rex better than anyone, his testimony was ignored by the prosecution and the investigators. He, dozens of others and I all maintained Rex's innocence right up to the end.

I still do...

*

After posting bond, Rex went to the small East Texas town of Tyler for arraignment before Judge William M. Steger. Rex entered a plea of not guilty to all counts of the indictment, and the case was set for trial on October 1, 1981.

On August 7, 1981, the Grand Jury returned a ten count indictment (Criminal No. S-81-15CR) under the umbrella of the Racketeer-Influenced and Corrupt Organizations Act. It was signed by Mozelle Card, Foreman. A warrant was issued and handed to the Deputy Marshall in Tyler.

Section B of 18 U.S.C. stated that "the District Courts of the U.S. shall have jurisdiction to enter such restraining orders or prohibitions in connection with any property or other interests subject to forfeiture under this section, as it shall deem proper." This provision was intended "to prevent the

pre-conviction transfer of property to defeat the purposes of the penalty provided by Congress."

This was what the government were after.

Rex's money…

Upon conviction, these provided for the forfeiture of all Rex's business interests which at that time amounted to over 100 million, and became the largest forfeiture in U.S. history.

It also represents the largest miscarriage of justice in the U.S. Rex was unable to access any of his assets except minimal living expenses

On October 5, the court set a gag rule on all parties. The only talking allowed to be done would be in court. As this was not done, Judge Steger eventually released two jurors for talking with TIME magazine on two occasions. On August 19, Judge Steger ordered that all parties and attorneys refrain from releasing any extra-judicial statements as this would interfere with the administration of a fair trial.

On August 28, a motion for the prosecution was made to disclose agreements between the government and the government witnesses. This was never disclosed, one of many missteps by the prosecution that made it impossible to expect a fair trial.

Rex waived his right to a speedy trial and the date was reset for January 11, 1982. All Rex's assets were frozen under the Racketeer-Influenced and Corrupt Organizations statute even before he had his day in court.

What happened to the constitutional right to being innocent until proven guilty? That certainly did not apply to Rex Cauble.

The case was undermined from the beginning by he government's agreements with Ray Hawkins, Larry Dale Washington and Willis Judge Butler which were never disclosed to the defendant, clearly an unlawful omission.

Furthermore, it was curious to me that all the other defendants' cases were lumped together and tried all at once. The motive was clear: Rex Cauble had the money - vast attachable assets - that the government was after. It became obvious that the U.S. Attorneys were after Rex and his fortune, not the real guilty parties.

The prosecution sought and received special funding to prosecute an innocent man.

As Rex once said, "It's all about money."

It certainly was.

*

As the news spread and the media had a field day, friends rallied to his support - people like Texas Governor John Connally, actor Dale Robertson, Judge Byron Matthews, Ruth Carter Stapleton (sister of U.S. President Jimmy Carter) and dozens of others who were horrified that Rex should be suspected of any involvement in the marijuana smuggling operation.

Rex's involvement with Muscles Foster stemmed purely from their employer-employee relationship, and nothing more, yet Rex was accused of loaning money to Muscles to finance the marijuana deals. Which was even more outrageous considering the fact that David Baugh had already tried Muscles and found him not guilty.

Which brings up the matter of "good faith indictments." If Muscles was found not guilty by a Federal jury after David Baugh's vitriolic prosecution, one could presume that Baugh's allegations against Rex were inspired by a "get even maneuver." Flimsy circumstantial evidence made the indictments highly suspect, none of which were based on fact.

It was claimed that Rex embezzled money from the two banks he owned. These counts resulted from loans that Rex made to Muscles for $50,000 to build and equip the Long Branch saloon in Denton. Rex was the surety on these loans and personally guaranteed them, just as he did on loans to myself.

But more important was the fact that $50,000 was small change to Rex Cauble, a man who was worth millions at the time. Bank records showed that

Rex repaid the loans after Muscles defaulted on the loans. The charges of embezzlement against Rex only underscored bad faith on the part of the prosecution. State and national bank examiners were unable to uncover any evidence of embezzlement.

One afternoon Rex and I were talking about this unfortunate development.

"Roy, it is possible for anyone to welcome this indictment," he said firmly, "Despite the embarrassment, expense and inconvenience of a public trial, I welcome this. For the past two years my privacy has been invaded by Federal investigators. My reputation has been severely damaged in the newspapers, periodicals and the electronic media through planted leaks. Now I am being indicted for something of which I am completely innocent."

I sympathized with him, of course. What else could I do other than stress my support of his innocence, just as all his close friends had done?

"Let me say further," Rex continued. "That the allegations that have been made publicly will now go to a fair and impartial jury in which I have faith. I will be completely vindicated and I have faith that the truth will prevail. Roy, I'm innocent and it will be proven."

He stared at me, his voice shaking with emotion and his eyes burning intensely. I truly felt for my friend at that moment, but had a disheartening feeling that it would not work out the way everyone thought it would.

I only wish his hopes for a fair and impartial trial had materialized. One wonders why David Baugh waited over two years to take the case to the Grand Jury. Rex was not even invited. No evidence had been produced. It was poetic justice that because of his actions, David Baugh ultimately became an embarrassment to the prosecutors and was subsequently transferred.

*

Rex's trial finally began on January 16, 1982. Roy Minton and Jack Gray represented Rex. David Baugh, of course, was the prosecution. His long-time pursuit of Rex Cauble was finally coming into the home stretch.

It was painfully obvious from the start that the handpicked jury did not consist of Rex's peers. They were all barely blue-collar types.

Present on an appearance bond of $250,000, the former Texas Aeronautics Commission Chairman was flanked by Roy Minton of Longview, Texas, and Jack Gray.

As events moved forward, Rex Cauble's indictment, trial and eventual conviction was considered by many, including myself, to be a black mark against the judicial system in the U.S. and a tragic event in the life of a totally honest man who was loved and respected by many.

*

As Rex's trial got under way,

Federal Judge Joe Fisher was kept busy shuffling reporters in and out of his courtroom to insure the jurors followed his orders not to disclose any accounts of the trial to the press.

Judge Fisher even went so far as to denounce the media from the bench.

"It is of continuing consternation to this court," he stated, "that the news media seem to have no concern whether this trial is fair, or serves the betterment of society. Insofar as their irresponsibility is concerned, they do not make a contribution to the betterment of society."

These were harsh words, admittedly, but fully justified considering the situation.

In his final argument, David Baugh urged jurors to remember his contention that the key charge was racketeering. He also urged careful consideration of the charges and take into account the credibility of the alleged co-conspirators turned prosecution witnesses.

"The only conspiracy here," said Attorney Mike Matheny, "is these government witnesses trying to get out of trouble."

This was an accurate statement that applied to the entire trial, and in particular to the first trial of the cowboys when the accused conspirators would have done or said anything to get themselves off the hook.

The four government witnesses were charged with various offenses, including conspiracy, possession of marijuana and possession with intent to distribute. It soon became obvious that the Federal attorneys had one goal in mind: to get Rex Cauble. The Judge had once commented "this is more like a circus than a trial."

For more than two years Federal investigators had shadowed Rex, grasping at straws to bolster their flimsy investigation. Eventually it became clear that they would have a hard time building a case if they relied on Muscles to say what they wanted -

namely, that Rex was part of the smuggling operation.

After the authorities moved in, Muscles had fled to Bolivia to avoid arrest. The prosecution knew only too well that without Muscles they would have nothing with which to build a case against Rex.

The DEA had financed Bolivian bounty hunters to find and extradite Muscles in the hope he could be persuaded to be a prosecution witness in exchange for leniency. This financing was illegal, but this only showed the lengths to which the prosecution went to pursue Rex and get their hands on his vast attachable assets.

The bounty squad finally apprehended Muscles in his stucco house outside of Santa Cruz, only twenty days before Muscles was due to become a citizen of Bolivia.

Muscles disclosed that the squad of bounty hunters, led by a tough armed colonel, arrived at his front door. They informed him he would be returned by Wednesday if he would accompany them. Muscles knew what was going on, and gave them no trouble. He said the colonel constantly prodded him in the ribs with his pistol as they left his house.

He was loaded into a small airplane and flown to La Paz, the capital of Bolivia. He was thrown into a dark cell without water, toilets or windows. He was held for seven days, and was only given coffee to drink.

After seven days the colonel who arrested him returned and took him to the airport where Bolivian authorities purchased a commercial airline ticket to Miami, Florida, using DEA funds.

Muscles was handcuffed and taken onboard by a DEA agent.

Upon his arrival in Miami, Muscles was arrested and jailed.

A DEA agent came into the cell and told him if he attempted to escape, he would be killed. Later Muscles admitted that while the DEA agents did not arrest him in Bolivia, there was always an agent nearby during his kidnapping.

During the trial of the cowboys, it was very clear that Muscles was not going to be coerced or scared into testifying against an innocent man who had been like a father to him. The prosecution's plan to involve Muscles certainly backfired after Muscles testified that Rex had absolutely no knowledge of the smuggling operation, nor did he participate in any of the activities.

The two prosecutors, David Baugh and John Hannah, the Chief Prosecutor for the Eastern District of Texas, had been at odds for many months over whether they should indict Rex or not. Baugh was rabid in his determination to go after Rex. His colleagues disagreed despite the fact that Baugh had coordinated the case from the start, but still there was no solid evidence against Rex. Finally Baugh had became such an embarrassment that after the trial, he was transferred to Richmond, Virginia.

During Muscles' trial, the prosecution had reversed its tactics when it became apparent that Muscles was going to speak the truth about Rex, no matter what. So it was decided to acquit Muscles on the grounds of insanity so he would be unable to testify at Rex's trial.

In brief, the case against Rex was falling apart, much to the dismay of the prosecution. They had anticipated Muscles being their ace in the hole. Instead he turned out to be the rope around their necks. So they had to get rid of him before he blew them totally out of the water. As a result, Muscles was found not guilty on the grounds of insanity.

Muscles Foster was crazy? No way. Muscles should have been a member of (SAG) screen actors guild, as he did a tremendous acting job.

I had spent too much time with Muscles on the ranch to believe this. I won't deny he acted a little crazy at times, but not enough to be found not guilty on a plea of insanity. He would not let Rex take the fall for something he did not do, which certainly illustrated he had more than a lick of sense left in his head. Muscles remained steadfast and faithful to Rex, whereas his fellow smugglers did not.

Larry Dale Washington, Willis Judge Butler and Charles Talkington were all desperately afraid of what might happen to them, and would have said anything to extricate themselves from the mess they were in. They may have been scared but Muscles was not. He certainly enjoyed the notoriety he achieved, something he had always coveted. I remember many times before the smuggling operation was closed down, Muscles loved to boast, especially to women, that he was a Marijuana smuggler.

He *was* a drug smuggler, but ne loved and respected Rex Cauble too much to rat on him and give statements to the prosecution that were untrue.

That old saying "Ye Shall Know the Truth and the Truth shall make you Free" certainly held true with Muscles. After the cowboy trial, Muscles was free, and down the line, Rex Cauble was convicted, but not through any false statements from Muscles. Crazy or not, he remained faithful to his old friend and father figure and told the truth.

Muscles was certainly involved in the Cowboy Mafia but Rex Cauble was not.

CHAPTER 13

Looking back over the weeks of Rex's trial, I remember many things that in retrospect seem unbelievable, especially the actions of the prosecution witnesses like Larry Dale Washington, Willis Judge Butler, Ray Hawkins and Les Fuller.

Larry Dale tried without success to change his statement, saying that he had no knowledge that Rex was involved in the smuggling operation.

In a tape recorded statement to his lawyers, Randy Schaffer and G. Brockett Irwin, Larry said his original statement two years earlier read differently than it should have. He also claimed that he asked one of the investigators to change his statement, but the investigator refused, claiming it would be too much trouble to retype the document.

Larry commented: "This is a fair example of the tactics deployed by the prosecution as well as the investigators."

Before he died out on Lake Tyler, Brockett Irwin, who was as well known and respected as Racehorse Haynes, felt confident that Rex would be cleared and showed some skepticism over the entire investigation.

I remember once we were standing outside the courthouse and Irwin said to me: "Roy, I don't think the investigative agencies are in a position to suggest they've been acting in error and that they have wasted the investigative expenses. But let me say that I've never known a man who's had greater courage than Rex Cauble in the face of a storm."

I also remember feeling a surge of sickening concern over the possibility that Rex would be wrongfully convicted. Our judicial system may be the best in the world, but it's far from perfect, especially when the stakes are high. As Rex said to me once, "This is all about money." Getting their hands on Rex's millions were the underlying motivation for the prosecution.

Which was so true considering the ultimate outcome: Muscles was acquitted, Rex was convicted; so it became clear that the prosecution was dancing around the laws of the land, all in the name of big money.

U.S. Marshal Clint Peoples recalled that only two weeks before Les Fuller died in the plane crash, he had recanted his statement to DEA agents that Rex knew about the cowboys' activities.

Peoples said that Fuller had come to his office with his attorney, Jim Rolfe, to talk about surrendering himself in Dallas rather than make the trip to Beaumont.

Peoples stated: "Let me make it clear, Les was not being interrogated or asked any questions, but out of a clear blue sky, he brought up Rex's name. The man had tears in his eyes and said he thought Rex was getting a raw deal. Rex is no more guilty of this charge than you or I," Fuller concluded tearfully. "I hate this worse than anything because we are the ones who are guilty."

Peoples went on to say that he had known Rex since they met in the Conroe, Texas oilfields in the 1930's.

"I did not solicit any of the statements from Fuller," he continued firmly. "I never asked him one question at the beginning and never asked him one question at the end. I have never told anyone of this, but it has been something that I felt should be confined to this office."

It was true that all of the prosecution's witnesses tried to recant their damaging statements that were given some years prior to Rex's trial.

I had known Larry Dale, Willis Judge and Les Fuller for many years, and truly believe they could not live with their conscience if they did not tell the truth; and after the initial shock of their arrest wore off, they would have been willing and prepared to tell the whole truth had they been given the opportunity.

It's a sad commentary on the system that they were never given that opportunity. I recall the many instances when they all talked with me, and all confessed they simply had to tell the truth.

My son, J.R. was close friends with Les' youngest son, Mitchell, and we all visited together many times during that period between the cowboys' trial and Rex's trial. Les often told me he felt horrible at having succumbed to the intense pressure and persuasion of the DEA and the FBI. Les had already

plea-bargained for a six month sentence, after which he seemed to regain some of his swagger and was not so scared any longer. Which was understandable as Les and Rex had been longtime friends and Rex had helped Les many times through the years.

*

I've never forgotten the last visit I had with Les Fuller at his ranch in Aubrey, Texas. Les confessed he had let greed ruin his career and that he had hurt many people in the process.

He tearfully described the risks they had endured and the anxiety and uncertainty that it all produced.

"Roy, how could I have got involved with that mess?" he said as the tears rolled down his cheeks.

"I've let down a lot of people. It wasn't worth it. The risks we took were crazy. We were insane. Many times I thought we wouldn't make it back because of the storms. The last trip nearly scared me to death. The shrimp boat was tossed around in those rough seas and if that wasn't enough, on the journey back in the "Jubilee" we were approached by Colombian pirates just as we were leaving Colombian waters. We were prepared with 50-caliber automatic guns, they were unsuspecting. We blew the hell out of their 20-foot boats and sailed on. We unloaded multiple rounds into the hull of the pirates' boat. They learned quickly about the "Cowboy Mafia." They most likely sank. The pirates would have taken the entire cargo if they had been successful. It was the scariest thing I've ever endured. At that point it just wasn't worth it."

I got the impression that Les was truly remorseful for the problems resulting from his involvement in the smuggling operation.

This visit was about a month before Rex's trial. Two weeks later Les's plane crashed in the Corpus Christi bay. All aboard were found except Les Fuller.

After about a week of fruitless coastguard searches I decided to help. My son, J.R. and I towed our Wellcraft 255 south and trolled the Corpus Christi bay for two days. The waters were rough and treacherous but we continued for two days without success.

A commercial fisherman finally found Les' briefcase floating about two miles off the coast. About a day later another fisherman found Les' body floating in the water. As always, he was wearing a lot of expensive jewelry, which was common for the "Marlboro Man."

I remembered that Les told me in no uncertain terms that he was going to tell the truth regarding all the activities of the "Cowboy Mafia" but sadly, he never had that opportunity to establish the fact that Rex Cauble was not involved in drug smuggling.

After Les' body was recovered there was increased uncertainty regarding the trial. The level of coercion by the authorities was staggering to me. After my many talks with all the cowboys, I felt that Rex would eventually be treated fairly, but I was mistaken.

*

I remember one night when I had dinner with Rex at his house, just a short distance from my home on Ganzer Road. We got into a discussion about the indictment. I told Rex I had no doubts about his innocence.

"It'll be proven in a court of law," I said, hoping to perk up his spirits. He had been understandably very tense, quite understandable in anyone who had been erroneously indicted on ten Federal counts.

Little did we know that the courts would be exercising arbitrary power rather than going by the rule of law, which had already been evident in the trials of the cowboys.

Rex nodded glumly. "I appreciate your confidence," he replied, "But it's obvious to me what they're after. I've done nothing wrong, but the prosecution is bound and determined to sink me. I've worked hard all my life and it's really disheartening that they now want to take it all away. I've always treated folks the way I would want to be treated. I've given an awful lot to folks who were less fortunate. This whole thing makes me sick. Even if I'm found not guilty, my reputation and the respect I've worked for is gone."

A wave of sorrow washed over me as I looked at his normally cheerful face now creased with grave concern.

"You know, Roy, never in a million years would I jeopardize what I've built. I have some of the most wonderful friends in the world, including you."

He leaned forward across the table and put a hand on my arm.

"You're much more to me that just my pilot, Roy. You're my trusted friend and confidante. I've always felt safe when we're in the air and you're up there behind the yoke, flying the plane. Remember the time when John Connally and I were in Houston and you were supposed to pick us up in the Kingaire?"

"Yes, I remember," I nodded.

He grinned. "You called and said there were heavy thunderstorms in the Houston area and felt it wouldn't be wise to pick us up in the Kingaire. I was mad as a hornet, and we had to take a commercial flight. That aircraft bounced around like a bucking bronco, and I knew you'd been right. After that I never questioned your decisions."

Rex paused a moment, his mind obviously going over the pending trial and what the outcome would be.

"I also appreciate the times you've checked up on Muscles for me," he continued. "That wasn't exactly part of your job as pilot. I'm certain the only reason they've brought Muscles back from Bolivia is to testify against me but I think they're going to be disappointed. Muscles will tell the truth. It still amazes me how my association with Muscles has got me into such a mess," he finished, reaching for his coffee.

He took a sip and looking at his expression, I again felt the depth of his anguish over the situation.

"In the end the truth will prevail," I said, hoping my voice carried the conviction that I frankly wasn't too sure about at that moment. "You'll be found innocent in the courts, Rex."

I tried to sound confident, but I think we both subconsciously knew that it might not work out the way we hoped. None of the cowboys told the truth, except Muscles, but that had been at the cowboy trial at which he was found not guilty because of insanity. The prosecution knew they could not call him to testify at Rex's trial because he would obviously tell the truth again and thereby destroy their flimsy case against Rex.

*

Prior to Rex's trial the investigators grudgingly admitted that their case had incurred some serious setbacks.

A review by the U.S. Justice Department revealed that the prosecution was not playing by the rules.

After the cowboys' trial, Irwin had stated: "I believe the government's zealous investigation is now on the wane. I don't consider any of the evidence to be strong at this hour. Examining the circumstantial evidence and comparing it with the testimony of the government witnesses, I can only draw the conclusion that Rex Cauble is innocent."

Irwin was a frank, matter-of-fact type of lawyer whose opinions were shared by us all. It saddened us all when we heard of his death out on the lake.

What we did not anticipate at that point was the arbitrary power and recklessness that would be used by David Baugh and the prosecution. Irwin often spoke of Rex's good points and once stated he was a far greater man than those pursuing him.

On one occasion in Rex's office, Irwin told me that the prosecution was too deeply committed to back off.

"Baugh can ill afford to back away from ill-advised statements," Irwin said and he was absolutely correct.

Rex confided to me that he was terribly hurt by the cowboys' lies. He had employed and fed these men, and did not expect them to say the things they did.

I personally felt terrible for Rex. He was an outstanding human being. He had tremendous courage, was kind, thoughtful, and he wound up being shafted by the men he had helped. Plus, the strong-arm tactics deployed by the government could have been expected under the circumstances, but it was tragic nonetheless.

The statements made by Larry Dale, Willis Judge and Ray Hawkins had all been coerced out of them by the government, yet they were not allowed to retract their words. This was yet another scary aspect of the entire trial. Willis Judge was even sequestered by the government because they believed they were losing their leverage over the cowboys. Many times I realized that bad things often happen to good people when money is at stake.

The affidavit by Lowell T. Miller, Ray Hawkins' banker in Valley View, Texas, describes in detail the tactics used by the government, who had forced him to testify against Rex.

Ray said that the FBI agents

told him if he did not testify against Rex, the government would try him on three separate felony counts, one at a time, and his wife, Karen, would be arrested and prosecuted. He had no choice but to do what the government forced him to do. He did not have the money for a new trial on his reversed conviction and certainly not to stand trial on three separate felony trials he was threatened with. The government had frozen Ray's assets just as they had frozen Rex's. Mr. Miller stated that he was shocked by what Ray told him and he was not alone. I became more and more disgusted as day by day events moved forward toward Rex's inevitable conviction and imprisonment.

*

It was more than surprising to me, Rex and his attorneys that the government admitted Ray Hawkins' testimony in Rex's trial. I believe even the jury was shocked that his testimony was deemed admissible. When this statement came out, I realized Rex's concern escalated. When Ray was confronted under cross-examination with the blatant testimonial inconsistencies, Ray admitted perjuring himself time and time again before the Grand Jury. He was not prosecuted for this, nor was he given any indication that he would be, which made it all highly suspicious.

From the onset of the investigation into the Cowboy Mafia, plus the many visits from FBI Agents Grimes and Masterson, I was expecting to be subpoenaed. I welcomed this as I knew I would be the one person who would tell the truth. As the cowboy trial proceeded, it was obvious that there was little but flimsy circumstantial evidence against Rex.

With the exception of Les Fuller, all the cowboys were not to be sentenced until after Rex's trial to insure they cooperated with the government. I thought this more than underhanded, but David Baugh and the prosecution had their agenda in place. The witnesses were quarantined, and the venue set in the barely blue-collar town of Tyler in East Texas. Major magazine reporters flooded into the town and we were all put up at the local Holiday Inn. It made me think of an armed camp - the prosecution on one side of the hotel, and the defense on the other. Rex felt confident he would win out and be acquitted as innocent of the charges against him. But it was more like a rigged heavy-weight fight.

On that crucial day, January 12, 1982, Rex was accompanied by his attorneys, Jack Gray and Roy Minton as well as his pastor, Dale Jackson. I went with him at 9 a.m. that day, and we were appalled at the media crush on the way to the courthouse. The entrance and hallways were clogged with reporters, eager to take pictures of Rex, who was dressed in his trademark Cutter Bill Western attire: a western suit, cowboy hat and alligator boots.

Cameras flashed at us every step we took, and once we were seated, the first order of business was for the county clerk to read instructions to the jury. U.S. Attorney John Hannah and U.S. Assistant Attorney David Baugh were seated on opposite sides of the courtroom, and it was obvious there was no love lost between these two men. I hardly ever saw them speak to each other.

The jury was obviously not the brightest group of men judging from their appearance and expressions. These good ol' boys were mostly employees of the Tyler Steel and Pipe Company. I suspected that not one of these men would believe that Rex had accumulated his wealth honestly.

Rex entered an official plea of not guilty on all counts of the indictment.

CHAPTER 14

As the trial proceeded, the jury paid more attention to the media than to the statements of the lawyers or witnesses.

Jack Gray leaned over to me and whispered, "Roy, I don't believe any of these jurors are peers."

I had to agree. The court had a tough time holding their attention, and after the Judge's patience began to wear thin, and he forcefully spoke to the jury.

"I ask you pay close attention to my remarks," he began. "It is a well recognized principle that every person charged with a violation of the law is presumed innocent until proven guilty, and the burden rests with the government to establish to your satisfaction beyond any reasonable doubt that the accused is guilty as charged. This presumption of innocence remains with the defendant until there is proof that satisfies you that the presumption of innocence no longer remains. So you must all look to the evidence introduced in this case, and ask yourselves whether or not you are satisfied beyond reasonable doubt that the offense has been committed as charged in the indictment. If so, it will be your duty to convict the defendant. But if reasonable doubt exists in your minds, you must give him the benefit of the doubt and acquit him."

I thought that would be the end of the Judge's lengthy spiel, but he continued, with the jury growing more and more restive as his voice rang out in the crowded courtroom.

"If there are two reasonable theories equally supported by the evidence, one of which is consistent with the guilt of the defendant, the other consistent with his innocence, then you must adopt that theory consistent with innocence and acquit him because it cannot be said he is guilty beyond reasonable doubt."

I considered the irony of this statement because Rex's assets had been frozen long before his trial, indicating that he was presumed guilty until proven innocent.

It was very clear that the jurors did not understand the Judge's instructions as their attention was totally consumed by the flood of reporters. Eventually the media reporters were removed from the court after Judge Steger commented that the trial was turning into a circus.

The Clerk of the Court began his

spiel: "Members of the jury, I have some instructions and definitions that will apply to the trial of this suit: s-81-15-CR, United States of America vs. Rex C. Cauble."

As the monotonous voice droned on, my mind fled back to the many good times Rex and I had enjoyed together - the Superbowls, the heavyweight fights, the new years celebrations and my heart bled for this wonderful friend who was being so unfairly prosecuted by his country who were obviously only after his massive fortune under the arcane laws of the Racketeer-Influenced and Corrupt Organizations Act, USC, 1962. And considering the good that Rex had done, the many people he had helped over the years, it was unbelievable that he was being tried on ten superficial counts.

Roy Minton filed a motion to have the venue moved to a locale where a jury could be chosen from people on the same level as Rex instead of the working class types to be found in Tyler.

During the trial Rex often looked over at me and his attorneys and would shake his head in disbelief. I was so sorry for him, and felt so helpless. I could do nothing but stand firm and tell the truth when my turn came to take the stand.

In addition to having repeatedly perjured himself, through a favorable plea bargain agreement, Ray Hawkins had strong incentives to bias his statements in favor of the government because of a favorable plea bargain agreement that was never disclosed to the defense. This was yet another illustration of the unfair tactics employed by the prosecution. There was endless head-shaking among us as the trial moved on to become a total farce.

Ray Hawkins was facing the threat of a new trial at which he would have received twenty years in prison following the reversal of an earlier conviction. Ray testified that he never had any conversations with Rex at his house which was totally inconsistent with Larry Dale Washington's earlier statement that had been pried out of him by the prosecution.

Ray was to have all counts dismissed and he would also benefit by the release of a $100,000 government lien on his Cherokee Ranch in Valley View, Texas. At the time Ray had a contract of sale for a million dollars on the ranch which would net a handsome profit for him and Karen in exchange for testifying for the prosecution. He would also not be required to pay all the taxes on the sale of the ranch. Again, this illustrates the devious and unscrupulous way that the government handled this case.

Roy Minton did a great job bringing this to light but considering the simple hand-picked jury, his words fell on deaf ears. They all totally disregarded (or failed to understand) the witness credibility instructions. Ray Hawkins was an admitted impeached witness as he had perjured himself to the Grand Jury, and he admitted this. By law, testimony from any perjured witness is inadmissible as evidence, something that was not observed in Rex's trial.

Judge Steger stipulated, "It is the duty of the attorney on each side of the case to object when the other side offers testimony or other evidence which the attorney believes is not properly admissible. Upon allowing testimony or other evidence to be introduced over the objection of an attorney, the court does not, unless expressly stated, indicate any opinion as to the weight or effect of such evidence. When the court has sustained an objection to a question addressed to a witness, the jury must disregard the question entirely, and may draw no inference from the wording of it, or speculate as to what the witness would have said if permitted to answer the question. Now this concludes my preliminary remarks. At the conclusion of this case the court will give you a detailed oral charge as to the laws governing the facts in this case."

At this point Roy Minton turned to me.

"There's no way this jury can understand these instructions," he said quietly, his face grim and his voice carrying all the disgust that we both felt.

I agreed. During the entire instruction phase, the jury seemed totally dumbfounded and simply stared blankly at Rex.

Rex's face showed his deepening concerns.

"Where did they find this jury?" he asked me. "They don't want Muscles here to testify, and you and I both know that while Muscles is half-crazy, he darn sure is not insane. And for him to be acquitted by reasons of insanity shows clearly that the prosecution did not want his testimony in the courtroom."

And so we were forced to sit and endure the endless legal procedures that often made little sense. The truth is always believable yet many of the untrue the statements made during Rex's trial were regarded as the truth, which they were not. The entire trial was rigged, and Rex was the fall guy., and all because the government was after his millions.

*

Roy Minton labeled the extensive probe as "bureaucratic egomania" and blasted federal investigators for dragging out the mention of an indictment for so long.

"What can Assistant U.S. Attorney David Baugh do," he asked the group of reporters outside the courthouse, "to right what he has done to besmirch Rex Cauble's good reputation? This is a case where the government looked around, found a Horatio Alger, saw an Alger Hiss and tried to prosecute an Alger Hiss," he added caustically.

As Rex and I stood on the steps of the courthouse discussing the early events of the trial, Minton told reporters he had developed evidence during his investigation that proved Rex's innocence. Part of this was a statement that Les Fuller gave to Federal investigators.

Les told U.S. Marshal James Peoples that Rex did not participate or have any knowledge of the smuggling operation. Minton went on to say, "I have developed evidence that raises serious questions concerning witness intimidation, attorney harassment and perjury."

After the Grand Jury proceedings prior to Rex's trial, U.S. John Hannah was against any indictment of Rex, something that put him at cross purposes with David Baugh. John Hannah, the top law enforcer in the Eastern district of the country, was Baugh's superior, which was the reason that Baugh was transferred after Rex's trial.

Plain and simple, Baugh had talked too much to back down. Two years earlier, referring to a possible indictment of Rex, Hannah said he did not believe Baugh had anything warranting an indictment, something that was stated quite aggressively.

It became evident throughout the trial that Baugh had embarrassed the U.S. Attorneys office administration. Baugh operated as if he had something to prove, and this did not reflect positively on the U.S. Attorney's Office. This was indicative of the entire criminal justice system being in disarray. The indictment of Rex became a political, not a legal issue, and David Baugh fully understood that Rex's innocence was a political liability to his burgeoning legal career.

Roy Minton had concrete irrefutable evidence of Rex's innocence, something with which U.S. Attorney John Hannah agreed without question. Hannah stated he felt Rex had been "drawn into the fray."

From the very onset of the investigation, Hannah and Baugh butted heads over the integrity and quality of the evidence in Rex's case. The investigators had not found the truth. The U.S. District Attorneys failed to uncover the truth. It was only the jury who could determine the ultimate truth.

After witnessing all the shenanigans in that courtroom, I came to the conclusion that juries should be given "innocence training" meaning they should be told that "you're doing this because we have to find the truth."

And there is *no* Innocence Commission in the United States that could study a case and possibly help reverse convictions of innocent people. Take the statistics on wrongful convictions: Mistaken eyewitnesses have been responsible for 83% of convictions, informants for 23%, false confessions for 22%, chump lawyers for 26%, misconduct of prosecutors for 44% and police misconduct for 51%. It is a poor reflection on our country that the criminal justice system is the only one that exempts itself from self-examination.

*

The trial moved forward, with both camps separate and divided at the Holiday Inn. Both were protective of their witnesses, with the attorneys careful they did not get out of their sight. The cowboy witnesses were not to go anywhere without supervision. They made sure I was not approached or questioned any further by the prosecution attorneys.

DEA agents Masterson and FBI agent Grimes spoke often to Ginger and me, always dropping in around dinner time. On many occasions they questioned me about flight records, flight plans and fuel receipts; but I was never apprehensive or nervous as I knew Rex had done nothing wrong. I've never been easily intimidated, and though they often tried to have me make certain statements, I simply told the truth. They finally realized I was not going to be coerced or intimidated in any way and their visits became less frequent.

Rex, Jack Gray and Roy Minton were next door to Ginger and me in the Holiday Inn. Every night over dinner at the local diner we would discuss the day's events. We constantly had to try and escape the news media who were holed up outside our rooms. It was difficult leaving the hotel and trying to avoid the mob of news reporters who were only doing their job, but the constant harassment did become annoying. They were looking for any kind of statement, and we had to keep quiet because we had been instructed on the first day of the trial that no one was to talk to the press.

A few jurors could not resist and were warned by Judge Steger. In fact, two jurors were released after repeated warnings. This could have resulted in a mistrial, as it often does. But there was too much at stake, given the fact that the prosecution's whole case depended on the plea-bargained cowboys and they were in constant fear of losing the leverage they had over Larry Dale Washington, Willis Judge Butler and Dayton Bud Evans. Their ace in the hole, of course, was Ray Hawkins, who was their only hope of a conviction.

Two years before Rex's trial, the cowboys had tried to retract their statements, but they were not allowed to change anything they had said like Les Fuller had done when interviewed by U.S. Marshall Clint Peoples. Les Fuller would have completely exonerated Rex had he not died in the plane crash in Corpus Christi some days before the trial. Les had already agreed to a six month sentence and was prepared to tell the truth.

In one of my many conversations

with Les at his ranch in Aubrey, Tex, he told me he was only intimidated for a short period.

"I cannot and will not allow Rex to take the heat for something he had no involvement in and no knowledge of," he said seriously. "Believe me, Roy, I think about this morning, noon and night. I understand the positions of the other guys but I do not agree with what they're doing. And I will not be bullied by those Federal investigators, DEA agents or that damn U.S. Attorney David Baugh."

I was proud of Les for being forthright and honest. I have never understood why they gave Les a pre-arranged

six-month sentence and not the other. I can only assume they did not want to be too dissident regarding their tactics with the cowboys.

CHAPTER 15

The second day of the trial saw the prosecution call Larry Dale Washington to the stand. Larry Dale had been over at my house with Muscles on many occasions. He was a simple, honest, down-to-earth cowboy from Balch Springs, Texas, who had tried many times without success to change his earlier statements.

It was obvious Larry Dale did not feel good about testifying, and appeared nervous and disturbed every time he was questioned. He looked scared to death and on several occasions the prosecution told him to relax.

It was clear he had been briefed on how to answer and it was patently clear their questions were worded so as to lead him into responding the way they wanted. David Baugh led him down the primrose path and Rex and I often shook our heads in disbelief at what we were hearing. Several times Minton objected to the line of questioning, calling it preposterous.

Larry Dale testified that he had known Muscles since 1972 or 1973, and that he was working for a publishing firm in Dallas, and also training horses at the same time.

When asked how he met Muscles, Larry Dale replied that he was renting a place from Kitten Haver in Garland, Texas, where Muscles was a ranch foreman. Larry Dale was asked if Muscles worked for anyone else.

"Not at that time," he replied. "He was gone a lot training horses."

The prosecution continued. "Did you have an occasion to discuss how much money Muscles was making busting horses?"

Larry Dale hesitated a moment before replying.

"Muscles was making more than I was. He had much more experience than I had. He was the best horse trainer I've ever seen. People knew him more than they did me."

"Did you ask him or did he tell you that he was supplementing his horse training income?"

Larry Dale replied nervously. "I asked him where he got all his money and he said he was hauling marijuana." Muscles had made millions but was unpretentious and concealed his wealth with the exception of his talking, but nobody believed it anyway. Muscles drove an old maroon El Camino pickup if he wasn't driving a gooseneck.

"Did he say who he was hauling marijuana for?"

Larry Dale replied. "He showed

me a newspaper clipping where they had arrested Ray Hawkins. Muscles had no qualms telling people what he did to make the money. At that time I had known Muscles about six months. He told me that he was smuggling marijuana the first time I met him, so this did not surprise me one bit. I did not believe him but he did tell me that the very first time we met at the Cutter Bill Championship Arena."

Larry Dale went on to say he had worked for Muscles on the ranch, hauling oilfield tanks and horses to Houston.

"Tell us how you first came to find out about the transaction?"

"Muscles just told me that if I wanted to make some money, I could help him unload a boat."

It soon became clear that Larry Dale's responses had been dictated and pre-arranged by the prosecution. As the exchanges between U.S. Assistant District Attorney David Baugh and Larry Dale became almost ludicrous,

Minton objected many times to the line of obviously pre-determined questioning.

Witness the following exchanges:

BAUGH: Did you ever, or were you ever taken somewhere to do some work on the truck or something like that?

LARRY DALE: Yes. I picked up the truck in Arlington, Texas.

BAUGH: Who told you to go pick up that truck?

LARRY DALE: Muscles.

BAUGH: Who took you out to it?

LARRY DALE: Well, I followed Muscles.

BAUGH: Who else was with him?

LARRY DALE: Willis Judge Butler.

BAUGH: In Arlington, Texas, where did you go?

LARRY DALE: To a Ramada Inn.

BAUGH: When you got to the Ramada Inn, what did you find?

LARRY DALE: A pickup with a camper on the back of it.

BAUGH: What was wrong with it, or were you able to determine at that time what was wrong with it?

LARRY DALE: The fuel filter. I replaced it and I took it to Denton to the Turner Ranch.

BAUGH: What was in that truck?

LARRY DALE: Marijuana.

BAUGH: How was it packed?

LARRY DALE: In burlap sacks.

BAUGH: Was the camper full?

LARRY DALE: Yes.

At this point, I saw Rex shake his head in disbelief. Larry Dale went on to state that he was paid five hundred dollars to repair the pickup and take it to the Turner Ranch. Baugh continued doggedly with his questioning.

BAUGH: When was the next time you had any meetings or discussions about marijuana smuggling?

LARRY DALE: A few months later in Houston.

BAUGH: Where did you go?

LARRY DALE: To an apartment on

Westheimer that was used for Cutter Bill's Western World employees and some out of town clients as a convenience.

BAUGH: What was discussed during that time at the apartment?

LARRY DALE: I did not discuss anything. I just ran errands, picking up hydraulic jacks and chains for the boat.

BAUGH: Did Muscles have you doing anything to get ready for the boat to come in?

LARRY DALE: Yes, we were putting miles on the trucks.

BAUGH: Why were you putting miles on the trucks?

LARRY DALE: I don't know for sure. I guess because we had them leased and Muscles wanted to look legitimate.

BAUGH: How many trucks did you have?

LARRY DALE: Two.

BAUGH: Who was driving the trucks?

LARRY DALE: Myself and Willis Judge.

BAUGH: Where was the first place you went to pick up a load of marijuana?

LARRY DALE: The first place was Savannah, Georgia. We leased the 18-wheel tractor-trailers at Hunsaker Truck Leasing in Dallas then proceeded to Oklahoma and loaded the truck with alfalfa hay. Me and Muscles then drove to Georgia and met up with Willis Judge, loaded up and drove back to Houston to the Crockett, Texas, ranch and left the trucks there. We picked up another truck at Crockett and went to High Island, Texas, where the boat was to arrive.

BAUGH: What was the name of the facility at High Island?

LARRY DALE: Thompson Seafood.

BAUGH: What was the name of that vessel?

LARRY DALE: The Jubilee.

BAUGH: Tell me the condition at Thompson Seafood at that time. How close were they able to get the boat in?

LARRY DALE: It lacked about twenty feet getting to the dock. The water was too shallow.

BAUGH: What did you get off that boat?

LARRY DALE: Marijuana.

BAUGH: How much?

LARRY DALE: Forty thousand pounds in forty pound bales. The best grass this country has ever seen. Colombian Red Bud.

BAUGH: How long did it takes to unload forty thousand pounds?

LARRY DALE: About eight hours because we had to carry it so far. The boat and the truck were far apart.

This type of questioning went on and on about the marijuana being distributed from the Crockett Ranch, a clear indication that the cowboys had been very clever in their operations. But however bold and brazen the cowboys may have been, Larry Dale's body language clearly showed how uncomfortable he was on the stand. Many of his statements were redundant.

All the while, the jurors were obviously

pre-occupied with the media and with Rex. The truly damaging testimony came later from Ray Hawkins who clearly had the most to lose if he did not cooperate with the prosecution.

*

Under the Racketeer-Influenced and Corrupt Organizations Act, a defendant would have to have the intent required by the predicated offenses. Each count of the indictment against Rex required that he had guilty knowledge or intent (mens rea) in order to sustain a conviction. In counts 4,5, and 6, specific intent to promote an unlawful activity had to be shown.

Each side claimed the overall issue was whether Rex knew beyond reasonable doubt that his employees were engaged in marijuana smuggling. The evidence was insufficient to sustain a conviction, and the verdict was contrary to the weight of the evidence.

By far the most damaging testimony against Rex was given by Ray Hawkins, who claimed that he had told Rex he was a drug smuggler and had discussed drug smuggling in Rex's presence. He also stated that he had smoked marijuana in Rex's presence, and had given it to his friends. I personally know this was untrue and preposterous.

Ray also testified that he had a conversation with Rex after the bust of the Agnes Pauline, and Rex said he did not care what happened to all those involved. This evidence was admittedly inculpatory, but its value should have been discounted by Ray Hawkins' utter lack of credibility.

Ray was thoroughly impeached on cross-examination by sworn Grand Jury testimony he had given previously under a grant of immunity. During the Grand Jury testimony, he stated he did not have any conversations with Rex and did not know him that well, and had never had any conversations regarding marijuana smuggling.

When faced with the blatant testimonial inconsistencies, Ray admitted perjuring himself time and time again before the Grand Jury. He ultimately admitted he had lied about Rex having any knowledge of the smuggling activities. Unfortunately, this was not even taken into consideration as it should have been when considering the verdict.

Without Ray's testimony, the case against Rex contained little more than weak circumstantial evidence that could not have been consistent with Rex's innocence, and should not have prompted the ultimate verdict against Rex. The evidence consisted mainly of his relationships with Muscles, Ray Hawkins and Carlos Gerdes, plus the widespread use of Rex's property from which their loads of smuggled marijuana were distributed; and Rex testified that he had not visited some of his ranches for twelve years or more. There was absolutely no way for him to have known what was going on at these properties.

He left the running of the ranches to Muscles, who was required to report any matters to Rex. I felt even back then that Rex put too much faith in Muscles, but this was understandable. Their close bond spurred Rex always to make Muscles feel wanted and important.

Rex was surprised and disappointed that Ray Hawkins' testimony was admitted. As Ray took the stand, I was sitting with Rex. He turned to me and whispered: "Roy, Ray has admitted to perjury. This is home cooking if I have ever seen it. They're trying to hang me."

I couldn't have agreed more.

After Ray Hawkins' testimony, Rex's mood changed. He became increasingly quiet and subdued. He still went for his usual morning run to help relieve the stress, and as the trial proceeded, Rex's runs became longer and longer. He would typically wake up at five a.m., go for his usual run before going to his office to attend to business the rest of the day. In all my years with Rex, if I ever wanted to talk to him, I knew I could always find him at his office. This man's work ethic was admirable. He operated out of his office; but naturally, with the trial in progress, he had to go to the courthouse.

After the trial began, I would wait for him each morning and we would drive together to the courthouse together with Rex's attorneys and his pastor.

All through the trial, I felt the jury was constantly distracted by the media and the character witnesses - highly reputable individuals like former Texas Governor John Connally, Ruth Carter Stapleton (sister of President Jimmy Carter), Judge Byron Matthews and many other prominent Texans who came to lend support to a man they felt, as I did, was being unjustly accused of something he would never do.

Testimony given by Ray Hawkins, Larry Dale Washington and Willis Judge Butler was constantly conflicting. Impeachment material always concerns prior inconsistencies in statements made by a witness or matters that affect a witness' credibility.

Yet the government failed to show that Rex had conspired to conduct the alleged enterprise through a pattern of racketeering activity, as he was charged under the Racketeer-Influenced and Corrupt Organizations Act. Their attempts did not come close to proving that the Cauble enterprises were tainted with racketeering.

I eagerly awaited my turn on the stand, anxious to speak and give straightforward answers to their questions, which included the flight records and the names of passengers who flew on Rex's plane. I told the truth, and only wish the cowboys had done the same.

We all felt confident that Rex would be acquitted and shown to be the innocent victim he was.

*

As the trial moved inexorably toward the verdict, it became obvious that the prosecution had planned to have their witnesses say exactly what David Baugh wanted them to say in order to confirm Rex's involvement in the COWBOY MAFIA and to secure a conviction. Whether the statements were true or not seemed irrelevant. The prosecution was out to get Rex by fair means or foul.

Rex once commented to me that he felt Larry Dale Washington had become a professional government witness. Larry Dale must have felt the same when, under cross-examination, he himself said he had spent the better part of two years as a government witness. Certainly Larry Dale spent more time during those three years as a government witness than he did in any occupational pursuits.

The plea bargain between Larry Dale and the government had been sweetened on two occasions, with the penalty starting with a possible life sentence if convicted, moving to an agreed five year sentence, later down to two years then to six months if Larry Dale said what he was told to say on the stand. The same game was played with the Marlboro man, Les Fuller. Les had a pre-arranged sentence that was not dependent on the outcome of Rex's trial. And whatever Larry Dale's sentence turned out to be would only be determined after Rex's trial was over.

Under cross-examination, Minton asked Larry Dale:

"Mr. Washington, is it a fair statement to say that the government agreed to a six-month sentence and the Judge refused to accept Mr. Baugh's recommendation?"

Larry Dale agreed and Minton continued doggedly.

"And at that point in time when the Judge stated that the sentence recommended by the government was too light and imposed a greater sentence, the government moved to dismiss the indictment against you?"

Again Larry Dale agreed.

"And in fact," Minton went on, "they appealed it to the Fifth Circuit Court of Appeals on your behalf, joining the defense in an unusual and unorthodox prosecutorial stance? Is that a fair statement?"

Once more Larry Dale agreed.

"And throughout the long and tortured procedure of litigation, Mr. Baugh, the government agents and the government prosecutors were on your side?"

"Yes."

"They in fact prosecuted or aided in the prosecution of the appeal for you?"

"Yes, sir."

"And it would be a fair statement that the questions that Mr. Baugh asked you today were the same questions he asked you at those other trials, to the point that he didn't even need notes to ask you the questions today, did he?"

Larry Dale shook his head. "No."

"And if we might, to that limited extent, call it the government's script, your testimony on direct examination, followed the same testimony that you had given on direct examination in the earlier trials?"

"Yes."

"And yet you have told Mr. Baugh. and you have testified in court with respect to certain of these matters, wherein your opinion and your testimony gives a different judicial view to that expressed today. Would that be a fair statement?"

Once again Larry Dale had to agree.

"Your testimony today would be

inconsistent in spirit and in letter with that you have given on cross-examination in earlier trials?"

"Yes, sir."

Minton forged ahead, his voice growing louder and more accusing.

"And there is no denying that you have testified in court that in your opinion Mr. Cauble had no knowledge or involvement in marijuana smuggling?"

Larry Dale answered without hesitation. "I did not think that he was."

"And you told Mr. Baugh that?"

"Yes."

Minton paused a moment before moving on with a new thought.

"Let me ask your opinion concerning the ability of Ray Hawkins to tell the truth and your opinion is that he is not truthful and is not deserving of belief?"

Larry Dale hesitated. "Well, he might be telling the truth and he might not. I would not believe everything he says."

"All right. Can you tell me, based on your knowledge and experience, one government witness who has served one day in the penitentiary?"

"Charles Talkington."

"Charlie Talkington became a government witness after he had pled, did he not?"

"Yes."

"Willis Judge Butler has never served a day in the penitentiary?"

"No."

"And you know that Willis Judge Butler was one of Muscles Foster's top aides?"

"Yes."

"And you have not spent a day in the penitentiary?"

"No."

"And Dayton Bud Evans, a government witness has never served a day in the penitentiary? In fact, he went through the same legal process you did?"

"Yes."

"Mr. Butler, Mr. Evans and Mr. Fuller, all government witnesses, were given the same plea bargain agreement that you were?"

"Yes."

"So it is a fair statement that Charles Talkington, of all the people involved in what has been commonly called the "Cowboy Mafia," was the least involved, wasn't he?"

"Yes."

"And Muscles Foster and Ray Hawkins of those that have been convicted, based on your knowledge and experience, were the most involved?"

Again Larry Dale hesitated.

"A lot moreso that me or anyone else, you know, in our group, the "Cowboy Mafia" as the government calls us."

"But there have been no secrets from any of the agents, Mr. Masterson, Mr. Grimes, Mr. Rasmussen or Mr. Wedeman, from the outset of the investigation, that the one man that they wanted was Rex C. Cauble?"

"Yes, that's who they wanted."

"From day one?"

"From day one."

*

It became obvious to all, especially after Larry Dale's cross-examination, precisely what the government and prosecution were after. It was not the "Cowboy Mafia." It was Rex and his millions He became less and less confident in the outcome as the trial and testimony wore on.

Once he leaned over to me and whispered, "Roy, this is unbelievable and a shame."

Roy Minton and Jack Gray exchanged glances and shook their heads in disgust. We all got up and stood in the foyer of the courthouse, waiting for the jury to return their verdict.

Minton echoed a thought that Rex had expressed earlier.

"Rex, this is some good old-fashioned East Texas home cooking. I hope the jury can see through this birds' nest."

*

Of course, as we awaited the verdict, I felt, despite certain lingering concerns, that Rex would be found not guilty, especially after such a prestigious character witness as John Connally had taken the stand to testify on Rex's behalf.

I've always remembered how this former presidential candidate and highly respected Governor of Texas stood, an imposing figure and a commanding manner who had the members of the jury lock their eyes on him as he spoke.

Connally had been, like Rex, a successful oilman who also had a very successful law practice. Together they had shared success in several oil drilling projects over the years. I considered myself fortunate to have met this great man several times whenever he and Rex would fly together to horse shows and campaign fund-raisers. Yet despite his cordial manner,

Connally had a strong sense of privacy, and always kept a certain distance from others.

On the stand, he spoke up with a firm, positive manner that underscored his aura of integrity and honesty.

"I pick my friends carefully," Connally said, his voice ringing out through the courtroom. "I watch them for a long time before I commit myself. I know I'm considered aloof. I have very few close friends, and I consider Rex Cauble to be one of them. Very few people know how to handle money and power, how to keep it from overcoming them. Rex is one that does handle it well. I have known Rex Cauble for many years and I know him well enough to know that he was not involved in any of this."

Despite John Connally's firm manner and impressive reassurances of Rex's innocence, I had a growing apprehension that the blue-collar jury would not relate to Rex and his high-profile character witnesses. It would be the old story of the have-nots being jealous and envious of the haves, resulting in a certain prejudice and an unfavorable verdict. Which was saddening for me because Rex was still a down-to-earth common man despite his enormous wealth and position. Rex never said a cross word to anybody.

CHAPTER 16

As we discovered early in the trial, the jury that was selected for Rex's trial obviously had a limited education and as a result, did not have the capacity to comprehend all the predicates under the Racketeer-Influenced and Corrupt Organizations Act, which are very complex. I felt that even the sharpest attorneys would have difficulty interpreting the rules and regulations governing those indicted under the Racketeer-Influenced and Corrupt Organizations Act, much less a jury of blue-collar workers that were sitting in judgment on Rex.

To ease jurors' task of determining guilt or innocence, the forfeiture issue should have been withheld from them until after they returned a general verdict. At the time of the trial the judge should have instructed jurors wholly about forfeiture and submit a special verdict to them.

In prosecuting under the Racketeer-Influenced and Corrupt Organizations Act, the forfeiture instructions to the jury did not make it appear that a conviction carried the penalty of automatic forfeiture of Rex's entire business assets. With all the media and high profile witnesses in the court, it was all Judge Steger could do to get the jury members to pay attention to his words, let alone absorb and understand his instructions.

Under the Racketeer-Influenced and Corrupt Organizations

Act, the government was required to prove that Rex conducted all his business affairs through a pattern of racketeering activity, which simply did not happen.

Rex, his attorneys and I were increasingly appalled at the way the laws of the Racketeer-Influenced and Corrupt Organizations Act were twisted to benefit the government case. Judge Steger should have made it clear to the jurors that only predicate acts alleged in the counts could support a conviction under the Racketeer-Influenced and Corrupt Organizations Act.

As we all waited for the verdict, Mr. Minton pointed out to Rex and me that a better practice in prosecuting under the Racketeer-Influenced and Corrupt Organizations Act would have been to reinforce instructions, stressing that the government had to prove two acts of racketeering activity beyond reasonable doubt and the jury had to be unanimous on each predicate. The laws of the Racketeer-Influenced and Corrupt Organizations Act are legalese at its finest, which were difficult enough for an attorney to comprehend, let alone that jury of blue-collar workers.

*

The testimony of Ray Hawkins was the most damaging to the defense. Ray was extremely tentative on the stand. It was obvious he did not feel very good about what he was having to do. As he had stated earlier to his banker, Lowell Miller, he was being led in his line of questioning.

On several occasions on the stand David Baugh had to remind Ray of what his earlier answer had been. I would tell that the jurors were perplexed by David Baugh more or less answering the questions for Ray, witness these few exchanges between government witness Ray Hawkins and Roy

Minton, defense attorney.

"If I may just make it clear for the court and the jury," said Minton ."I am now reading from the statement that was given to investigators by Ray Hawkins. 'This load on the Monkey was unloaded on trucks and taken to Cauble's ranch in Bosque County, Texas, and distributed. This load was backed by Carlos

Gerdes, Muscles and myself along with Charles Talkington. Have I read that correctly?"

Hawkins responded: "Yes sir, I am following you."

Minton continued. "Then let me back up a minute and read this again. This load was backed by...and here your initials are scratched out and then a comma and then some more is scratched out and then it says 'Carlos Gerdes and James Holland' - then something else is scratched out, then it says 'Muscles and myself along with Willis Judge Butler and Charles Talkington.' Let's read what was scratched out. Look at your copy, line three on page seven."

Hawkins: "I am looking at it."

"It says; this load was backed by John Ruppel."

"Righto."

"That is scratched out. Is that correct?" "Yeah, because I did not say that."

"And then later on it says Carlos Gerdes, James Holland. What is scratched out next?"

"Rex C. Cauble."

"Rex C. Cauble?"

"Right."

"And that is scratched out?"

"Righto."

"Who put those names in there?"

"I do not know. I scratched them out because I said I did not make that statement."

"Where was this typed up?"

"I do not know."

"At the FBI office?"

"I assume it was typed at the FBI office."

This was typical throughout Rex's trial. There was no continuity between the cowboys turned government witnesses.

After Ray testified, the mood seemed to change to guarded concern regarding the probable outcome. I was amazed that the jurors did not see through all this nonsense.

Toward the end of the trial a concerned look came over the faces of all of the defense. Certainly Rex and I found ourselves less and less optimistic. .The testimony of Willis Judge Butler had been tape recorded long

before Rex's trial. Willis had pleaded guilty and had become a key government witness.

After Willis failed to appear for a meeting with investigators, Federal agents issued a warrant for his arrest. Willis was apprehended and held for a time in protective custody. As the federal prosecutors pressed their investigation, Willis Judge became a crucial witness, testifying in three trials and appearing before

a federal grand jury investigating the Cowboy Mafia Operations.

While he was making court appearances to testify on behalf of the government, his attorney was appealing Willis' conviction, contending U.S. State District Judge Joe Fisher of Beaumont, Texas had acted improperly when he

denied a request by Willis to withdraw his guilty plea. The request to withdraw the plea came after Fisher refused to honor the plea bargain agreement Willis had struck with the government.

The Fifth Circuit Court of Appeals in New Orleans overturned his conviction and it appeared that Willis, despite his admitted part in the smuggling, would

be cleared of all charges. Prosecutors said he could be retried on the COWBOY MAFIA smuggling charges only if he

failed to live up to his plea bargain agreement by refusing to testify for the government.

Willis became the government's key witness in the trials of members of the Cowboy Mafia and Government agents leaned on him for every bit of information they felt was important.

All the coercion and the treatment was obviously too much for Willis Judge Butler. He shot himself prior to Rex's trial. Ironically, his death presented interesting legal questions, and his suicide helped federal prosecutors more than he could have had he lived to take the stand.

It was no wonder that Judge Steger dubbed Rex's trial a circus, marred as it was with all these types of shenanigans from start to finish.

*

Naturally we all had hopes of acquittal but after the jury deliberated for several hours, they returned a verdict of guilty. This unexpected outcome shocked

and surprised the defense, and many present in the courtroom wept when the verdict was read out.

Ruth Carter Stapleton was crying openly, and told me she had never in her life seen such dissident procedural deficiencies in any trial, or any court of law.

"Believe me, Roy, they'll get their karmic reward eventually," she said to me, wiping her tears away. Which was, ironically, a prophetic statement because David Baugh was eventually fired as assistant District Attorney.

I remember looking over at John Connally and his wife Nellie who sat stunned with their heads down.

I got teary eyed and gave Rex a hug.

"The appeal will go differently, Rex," I tried to console him, but Rex merely shook his head and smiled, a truly remarkable reaction to me.

Rex remained strong throughout

the entire trial, which only reinforced my enduring admiration of this courageous man caught in a web of circumstances beyond his control.

Rex was to remain on the same bond until the

appeal process began though he did have to put up an additional million dollars.

Between the time of the verdict and the appeal being prepared by Roy Minton, the mood at Cauble Enterprises was understandably somber. Rex tried to carry on business as usual but his assets were frozen and he was on a $5,000 a month allowance. Anything larger had to be approved by the Justice Department. This was a sad commentary in and of itself. There was certainly no justice served in Tyler, Texas in the case of the Cowboy Mafia and Rex Cauble.

Today my son J.R. is still close friends with Les Fuller's two sons, Michael and Mitchell. They have often said that if their father not died in that plane crash in Corpus Christi bay, he would certainly have been able to establish Rex's innocence; but sadly, the Marlboro Man didn't live to clear his good friend and save him from spending five years in prison and losing his fortune.

Those who were really responsible for the entire Cowboy Mafia operation got off virtually scot-free. Muscles, of course, had been found not guilty, and the other cowboys received light sentences in return for their coerced testimony. So compared with what happened to Rex, there was minimal punishment handed out to Larry Dale Washington, Charles Talkington, Dayton Bud Evans, Jamie Holland, Harry "The Hat" Hannon, Ray Hawkins and the Sneed family.

*

After Rex's trial things were very hectic and tense while the appeal was being prepared. Rex became somewhat discouraged but was still hopeful that the appeal would be successful.

I felt sorry for Rex because of all that must have been going through his mind. The appeal was based on the perjured witnesses, Ray Hawkins, the several procedural deficiencies, and the general tactics of the prosecution.

I shared Roy Minton's belief that the appeal would be successful but it was denied and Rex was to report to the Texas Federal Correctional facility in Big Spring.

The government had achieved the largest forfeiture in U.S. history and sent an innocent man to prison for five years.

*

June 4,1984 became one of the saddest days of my life.

I was to fly Rex to Big Spring, Texas.

It was a warm sunny day but the mood of the moment was anything but sunny as Rex said goodbye to all of the people he had worked with for many years. After several very emotional farewells, we left the Denton, Texas Municipal Airport at about eight o'clock for the short flight to Big Spring.

As we took off I could barely contain my feelings as Rex sat in the back of the plane, his face reflecting the sadness and disbelief shared by us all. I was especially moved when Rex and I began reminiscing about all the roads we had been down together.

When we arrived at Big Spring, the authorities were waiting to transfer Rex to the Federal Correctional Facility. I gave Rex a big hug and thanked him for the opportunity to work with him and for all the fun we had had over the years.

Rex had held up well for the most part, but at that moment of farewell, tears were glistening in his eyes as they were in mine.

"Roy Graham," he said in a choked-up voice. "I'd go down the river with you anytime. You're a good man."

Those were the last words Rex Cauble said to me on that fateful day when he left his world behind. In high-stakes games the innocent are sacrificed for the big prize. In this case the big prize was Rex's attachable assets under the arcane laws of (RICO), racketeer influenced corrupt organization. The prosecutor's "slop bucket." Ultimately, the simultaneous and consistent presentation of significant distortions in the news created misinformation synergies.

Chapter 17

Rex Cauble spent five years in Big Spring,Texas at the federal correctional facility and was a model inmate. This five year sentence certainly didn't fit the crime,this was certainly a light sentence for all that he was accused of. The attachable assets were the real target. Rex was seventy-three years old when he was released.Gone were the trapping of his immense wealth. The ranches, the banks, the western wear stores, the friends in high places, all gone. Rex had to start over. Forty years plus of oil drilling, ranching and banking...vanished. The golden horse, Cutterbill, Rexs' pride and joy had also died during this period. The number one sire of world champion cutting horses died at 22 years of age and left a great legacy.

This golden palomino was also a tremendous profit center for Cauble.I myself and my family had grown attached to Cutterbill..It seemed that Rex lost it all,all at once.Rex,at seventy-three was starting over.This time in the oil and gas trading business.No airplanes,no luxury items.Rex was a tough,determined,cowboy to have endured all of this and still have the will to dust himself off and get back in the saddle.I guarantee Rex found out who his real friends were when he was released from Big

Spring,TX.Rexs' horseshow buddy John Wayne had also passed during this period.The world changed quickly for this ole' cowboy.The cowboys Larry Dale Washington,Dayton Bud Evans,Jamie Holland,Ray Hawkins,the ones that were sentenced did 2-years.Larry Dale went to Ruidoso,New Mexico working horses,Dayton Bud Evans and Charles Talkington in Oklahoma in the horse and cattle business.Charles Talkington passed away recently in southeast Oklahoma.Ray Hawkins went to Ocala,Florida and breeds,trains and boards horses.Ray is one of the best horsemen in Florida.Ray knows horses.If i were looking for a horse i would look to Ocala,Florida and Ray Hawkins.My little buddy Muscles Foster was not sentenced and moved to Ruidoso, New Mexico as he loved the horses and the women.Muscles married a well to do women that was also in the horse business. Muscles loved to go out to Ruidoso downs for a little horse wagering then on over to the Texas club,Muscles favorite steak house anywhere.Muscles would sit in Rexs' club seats at Ruidoso Downs as the government didn't get these choice seats in the vip section. Muscles passed away about five years ago.I'll always remember Muscles Foster and that first night we met at the Cutterbill championship arena.We certainly had some good times.Muscles Foster was one of the best cowboys and actor i have ever seen as not a soul knew or believed what his extracurricular activities actually were.As country singer/songwriter George

Strait who has an abode in Ruidoso at Altos country club croons, this is truly where the cowboy rides away.